FRENCH COOKING

CHARTWELL
BOOKS INC.

Picture Credits:
Ole Brask 2;
Delu/Paf International 13; 20; 33; 37; 42; 43; 46; 50;
Alan Duns 8; 29; 45; 49; 54; 58; 60;
Bryn Cambell/John Hillelson Agency 1;
Paul Kemp 15; 16;
Don Last 32;
Max Logan 36;
Eric Lessing/Magnum 2/3; Elliott Erwit/Magnum 5;
David Meldrum 25; 56;
Stanli Opperman 12;
Picturepoint 4;
Roger Phillips 6; 7; 18; 19; 22; 26; 28;
31; 34; 39; 53; 55; 63;
Iain Reid 40; 46/7;
John Turner 11;

Cover: Roger Phillips.

Written and edited by Isabel Moore

Published by Chartwell Books Inc.,
a Division of Book Sales, Inc.,
110 Enterprise Avenue
Secaucus, New Jersey 07094

Parts of this material first published by
Marshall Cavendish Limited in the partwork *Supercook*

This volume first published 1977

Printed in Great Britain

ISBN 0 89009 103 X

Contents

Introduction

French cuisine is generally acknowledged, especially by the French, to be the best and most imaginative in the world. Any claims from Italy or China, who between them have contributed some of the history and many of the spices, are brushed aside. And the rest of the world, dazzled, agrees—even to the point of feeling faintly guilty if they DO prefer a plate of pasta to a pork noisette!

Perhaps what the French do have, in the end, is not so much a cuisine par excellence as an attitude par excellence. Time spent agonizing over menus, prodding vegetables to make sure they are of the correct ripeness, choosing just the 'right' cut of meat, then cooking all to perfection, is not considered to be time wasted as it so often is in the English-speaking world, but one of the most creative and useful ways of spending one's days. And it is an art as much practised by the suburban housewife as by the chef of a great restaurant. A difference in attitude which could be summed up by the treatment of leading chefs: in France they are showered with money, fame, honours, all the reverence that being the excellent exponent of a respected profession can bring, while in most of the rest of the world they are lucky if they earn a decent salary and are merely ignored.

There are two main and very distinct strands of French cooking. The first is *haute* or *grande cuisine*, practised since the beginning by a few very distinguished chefs, employed originally by royalty or the nobility but now more often

right: *A peasant family in the Dordogne have breakfast.*

far right: *Transporting the catch from the Marennes oyster beds off the coast of Bordeaux.*

by leading restaurants or hotels. The second is of course provincial or bourgeois cooking, the cooking of the regions and the people. The latter is what the people actually eat most of the time, the former what the heart (and that famous French liver . . .) aspires to.

The history of *haute cuisine* actually began in Italy, something the French somewhat gloss over, for until the sixteenth century the cooking of France was simple and rustic, with the accent on domestic meat and dairy produce. In the sixteenth century, however, the young Catherine de Medici came to France to marry the French king Henry II and with her she brought her cooks, steeped in the traditions of Renaissance Florence, and their creations, especially their pastries and ice-creams, revolutionized French cuisine.

Haute cuisine owes its prominence to a few giants, whose effect on even the cooking of everyday dishes has been profound. But even among the giants, two stand out: Carême who was the first, and Escoffier who was perhaps the greatest. Antonin Carême was born in 1784, one of twenty-five children, in a slum just outside Paris. Legend has it that at the age of eleven he was told to fend for himself and this he did by apprenticing himself in a local cook shop. Luckily his talents soon became evident

and he quickly became employed by the most famous *patissier* of the time, Bailly. One of Bailly's most distinguished clients was Talleyrand, and it was in his house that Carême really began his life's work—a career that was to see him as chef to Napoleon and to the Prince Regent of Britain (later George IV) among others (he cooked for him in his so-called cottage retreat at Brighton, an astonishing piece of architecture that closely resembled some of Carême's more ostentatious pastry *pièces monté*). He was, in fact, fascinated by design and at one point wished to be an architect, a preoccupation apparent in some of his *pièces montés* (set pieces), which he was in the habit of planning by sketching a series of blueprints. In between, he invented, amended, taught, wrote—and designed.

George Auguste Escoffier who was born almost a century after Carême, came from the south of France near Nice. When he was quite young he was among other things, an army cook (he cooked for the troops during the Franco-Prussian War when he apparently did rather wonderful things with horse meat). He then formed a partnership with César Ritz, the founder of the luxury hotel chain, and together they carried the message and reputation of the excellence of French food

as for the master chef cooking for a wide range of discriminating clients.

There were, of course, others who contributed greatly to the development of *haute cuisine*—Prosper Montagné, who wrote many books on the subject and who was the first to question the need for unnecessary embellishment, and Brillat-Savarin who was more gourmet than chef and considered himself to be a 'philosopher' of the kitchen. He wrote one of the most entertaining books on food ever published, *La Physiologie de Goût*, which is still widely read and translated today some 200 years after it was written.

The tradition goes on: in France the natural heirs of Carême and Escoffier are still at work, experimenting and shaping the cuisine to the needs of today. The leading exponents number about a dozen now and are called *La Bande* in France, and most of them own and cook in their own restaurants, which are located throughout the country. One of them, Michel Guérard, has even invented a new form, called *cuisine minceur*, which adapts the skills of *haute cuisine* to the reality of a low cholesterol life.

The 'other' cuisine of France is more modest—few fancy sauces or extravagant concoctions requiring architectural plans (although there is an area of overlap as the two different forms of cooking meet and learn from each other). Originally, many of the dishes were specialities of specific regions of the country. Most extol the virtues of patience and thrift, taking care to use even the most modest scraps, and using cheaper cuts of meat which are tenderized and cooked slowly to increase their succulence. And since France is a large country, stretching from dull, rainy northern coasts to sunny, southern Mediterranean ones, from the German border to the Swiss and from the Spanish to the Italian, the foods of these varying areas are in themselves very different from one another.

In the north there is Brittany and Normandy, lots of coast-line, rather rocky, which makes the seafood good and plentiful, and vast expanses of farmland which makes the meat, particularly the lamb, well regarded. In Brittany, one of the great delights is crêpes, purchasable for a few francs from road-side stalls and filled with anything from Grand Marnier to seafood. Normandy is farming country, lots of apple orchards, dairy produce, cream, butter and eggs, all successfully incorporated into the food, sharp dry cider and a brandy made from apples, called Calvados, which many connoisseurs consider

throughout the world. This was the era of the *belle epoque*, when eating out was not only fashionable but a social necessity and when the great restaurants and hotels, particularly of France and London came into their own. (Restaurants had been 'invented' just before the Revolution in France and must have struck a sympathetic chord in even that part of the population which could not afford them—despite the fact that the greater part of their natural clientele was wiped out during the Terror, they not only survived but prospered.) Paris and Monte Carlo, in particular, seemed to be populated solely by the beautiful, the gifted, the demi-mondaine and the gourmet, and Escoffier duly responded to the excitement of the time, naming several of his most popular creations in honour of actresses, singers or crowned heads of Europe. He did much more than immortalize Melba by calling that toast after her, however, for in addition to refining and simplifying some of the more grandiose ideas of Carême, he also remained true to his origins and incorporated into his repertoire, and therefore into the classical repertoire of France, many traditional dishes from the regions. His book *Ma Cuisine* includes several Provençal dishes, and remains as appropriate a guide for the housewife cooking for her family

right: *French wine is famous throughout the world—this particular vineyard is in one of the less well known wine areas of the country, in the Midi near Le Lavandou.*

far right: *An old man and a boy—a universal scene, yet typically rural French. The bread with pride of place on the back of the bicycle is the French staple, the* baguette.

finer than cognac. Normandy also produces what is probably France's most popular cheese, Camembert.

The Loire, Burgundy, the Rhône and Champagne are famous outside France mainly for their delightful wines, which number among the finest in the world. The cooking is excellent too—the *charcuterie* tradition flourishes in the Loire valley, especially around Tours, famous for its *rillettes*, a sort of potted pork, while Burgundian cooking relies on voluminous quantities of the native wine and is immortalized by *boeuf bourguignonne* and *coq au vin*. At Bresse, near Lyons, they consider their chickens to be the finest in France if not the world, and make many imaginative dishes with them.

Savoie is near to Switzerland, just across the lake from Geneva and so the Swiss influence is strong. The wines are white and somewhat flowery, the most commonly used cheese in cooking is Gruyère, and the food is unpretentious but filling. Chartreuse, the only liqueur still made by monks, is made in this region, and by the same order which first had that brilliant idea . . .

Alsace and Lorraine are usually held together by a hyphen and lumped together in the public imagination, although they are not that similar—in fact the main thing they have in common probably is that both, in their time, have formed part of Germany and have been batted back and forth by the two great

powers almost as the mood took them. Alsace produces some of the most delicate white wine in France, akin to the wines of the almost-neighbouring Rhine, and also some of the better French beer. The German influence is evident in the food too—in the popularity of sausages and smoked hams, and in the classic dish of *choucroute garnie*, the basis of which is sauerkraut. In Lorraine, there is that famous quiche—made in a thousand different ways, imitated to the point of unrecognizability, yet still absolutely delicious!

The southwestern border is significant too, for the Pyrenees, which separate France from Spain, house a people who refuse to belong to either, the Basques, who have their own language, customs—and cooking. Here there's lots of saffron, and dried red peppers, Spanish-style omelets and nourishing filling soups, many containing the traditional *confit d'oie* or pressed goose, and *daubes*, warming stews made from beef or lamb.

In the centre of France, there is Bordeaux, famous for its clarets and the best sweet white wine in the world, Sauternes, and the Marennes beds, noted for the excellence of their oysters and mussels. In the Périgord nearby, the local pigs help hunt out the precious truffle, which is so expensive now that delivery of a supply to a largish delicatessen requires a security guard.

Languedoc is different yet again. *Cassoulet* is probably the dish that is best known to the outside world and although there are many variations, a good one should include lamb or mutton, sausages and haricot (dried white) beans. In the south, the influence is Italian (Nice only became officially part of France during the Second Empire): lots of olive oil for cooking, and garlic and olives are almost part of the staple diet. Dishes are highly spiced and colourful and the southern herbs such as basil and rosemary are used with great abundance. In caves high above Marseilles, the blue Roquefort, made from ewe's milk, matures. A great deal of the *vin ordinaire* of France is now grown in this area, including some exceptionally pleasant dry white and rose wines.

The range is enormous and the taste superb—and the surprise is, when you cook even the more complex dishes, just how easy they are to create. And of course in a time of relative austerity the provincial dishes, with their ability to use almost every scrap in the kitchen, become an almost necessary addition to the repertoire of every budget-conscious cook.

Soups and Starters

SOUPE A L'OIGNON
(Onion Soup)

	Metric/U.K.	U.S.
Butter	75g/3oz	6 Tbs
Large onions, thinly sliced into rings	4	4
Flour	2 Tbs	2 Tbs
Salt and pepper to taste		
Beef stock	900ml/ 1½ pints	3¾ cups
French or Italian bread, cut approximately 1½cm/¾in thick and toasted	4 rounds	4 rounds
Garlic cloves, halved	2	2
Parmesan or Gruyère cheese, grated	75g/3oz	¾ cup

French Onion Soup, traditionally associated with the old Les Halles market in Paris but eaten and enjoyed throughout the world.

Melt the butter in a heavy flameproof casserole. Reduce the heat to low and add the onions. Simmer them, stirring occasionally, for 25 to 30 minutes, or until they are golden brown. Remove from the heat.

Stir in the flour and seasoning, then gradually add the stock. Return to high heat and bring to the boil. Reduce the heat to low, cover the casserole and simmer for 20 minutes.

Preheat the grill (broiler) to high.

Rub each bread round on each side with a garlic clove half, then discard the garlic. Float the rounds on the soup and sprinkle the cheese generously over the top. Put under the grill (broiler) and cook for 5 minutes, or until the top is golden and bubbling. Serve at once.

4 Servings

POTAGE PARMENTIER
(Potato and Leek Soup)

A version of this traditional country soup was adapted by the French chef Louis Diat to summer cooking. By chilling the soup over ice, he created one of the most popular of cold soups, Vichyssoise.

	Metric/U.K.	U.S.
Butter	50g/2oz	4 Tbs
Vegetable oil	2 Tbs	2 Tbs
Large onion, finely chopped	1	1

Medium leeks, white parts only, thinly sliced	3	3
Medium potatoes, finely chopped	6	6
Salt and pepper to taste		
Chicken stock	900ml/ 1½ pints	3¾ cups
Milk	300ml/10floz	1¼ cups

Melt the butter with the oil in a large saucepan. Add the onion and fry until it is soft. Stir in the leeks and potatoes and cook, turning occasionally, until the potatoes are evenly browned. Season with salt and pepper and pour over the stock and milk. Bring to the boil, stirring constantly. Reduce the heat to low, cover the pan and simmer for 20 to 25 minutes, or until the potatoes are very tender.

Pour the soup through a strainer into a bowl, using the back of a wooden spoon to rub the vegetables through. Discard the pulp in the strainer. Alternatively, purée the soup in a blender.

Return the soup to the saucepan and simmer for 5 minutes. Serve at once.

4-6 Servings

CONSOMME JULIENNE
(Vegetable Consommé)

	Metric/U.K.	U.S.
Butter	50g/2oz	4 Tbs
Carrot, cut into small thin strips	1	1
Celery stalks, cut into small thin strips	2	2
Potatoes, cut into small thin strips	2	2
Onion, chopped	1	1
Parsnips, cut into small thin strips	2	2
Canned beef bouillon	1¾l/3 pints	7½ cups
Salt and pepper to taste		
Dried thyme	½ tsp	½ tsp
Chopped fresh chervil or parsley	1 Tbs	1 Tbs

Melt the butter in a saucepan. Add the vegetables and reduce the heat to low. Cook, turning occasionally, for 15 minutes, or until they are just tender. Remove from the heat and

An elegant yet filling representative of haute cuisine, *Consommé Julienne.*

7

drain the vegetables in a colander. Set aside and keep hot.

Bring the bouillon to the boil over moderate heat. Add the vegetables, seasoning and herbs, and stir gently.

Serve at once.

6 Servings

SOUPE ALBIGEOISE
(Meat and Vegetable Soup)

This is one of the traditional soups of southwestern France. The confit d'oie or pressed goose, which is a specialty of the area, should be included if the soup is to be completely authentic, but since it is difficult to obtain outside France, it may be omitted.

	Metric/U.K.	U.S.
Beef ribs, separated	700g/1½lb	1½lb
Salt pork, diced	275g/10oz	2 cups
Bouquet garni	1	1
Beef stock	2½l/4 pints	5 pints
Dried broad (fava or lima) beans, soaked overnight in cold water and drained	225g/8oz	1⅓ cups
Medium green cabbage, coarsely shredded	1	1
Medium carrots, diced	4	4
Small turnips, sliced	4	4
Medium leeks, sliced	4	4
Large onions, sliced	2	2
Large potatoes, sliced	4	4
Garlic cloves, crushed	6	6
Garlic sausage, diced	½kg/1lb	1lb
Pressed goose (confit d'oie)	125g/4oz	4oz

Put the ribs, salt pork and bouquet garni in a flameproof casserole and stir in the stock. Bring to the boil, stirring constantly and skimming off any scum with a slotted spoon. Stir in the beans, reduce the heat to low and cover. Simmer the soup for 1 hour.

Increase the heat to moderate, add the vegetables and garlic and bring to the boil. Reduce the heat to low, re-cover and simmer for 1 hour.

Using a slotted spoon, remove the beef bones and bouquet garni from the soup. Cut the meat from the bones and return to the soup. Add the sausage and goose, and simmer the soup for a further 20 minutes.

Serve at once.

8-10 Servings

BOURRIDE
(Mixed Fish Soup)

This is one of the great dishes of Provence, almost rivalling the bouillabaisse in popularity. It can be made from almost any type of firm-fleshed fish but the important not-to-be-omitted essential of the dish is the aioli. If you want to cheat on making it, add three or four crushed garlic cloves to 300ml/10floz (1¼ cups) of commercially prepared mayonnaise. Boiled potatoes are also often added to the soup when serving.

	Metric/U.K.	U.S.
Firm white fish fillets (haddock, cod, John Dory, brill, or bass)	1½kg/3lb	3lb
Fish heads and trimmings from the fillets		
Water	1¼l/2 pints	5 cups
Dry white wine	300ml/10floz	1¼ cups
Onions, thinly sliced	2	2
Wine vinegar	2 Tbs	2 Tbs
Orange peel, blanched	7½cm/3in strip	3in strip
Bay leaf	1	1
Fennel seeds	1 tsp	1 tsp
Salt	1 tsp	1 tsp
French or Italian bread, toasted	6-8 rounds	6-8 rounds
AIOLI		
Dry breadcrumbs	1 Tbs	1 Tbs
Wine vinegar	1 Tbs	1 Tbs
Garlic cloves, crushed	4	4
Egg yolks	6	6
Salt	½ tsp	½ tsp
Dry mustard	¼ tsp	¼ tsp
White pepper	¼ tsp	¼ tsp
Olive oil	300ml/10floz	1¼ cups
Lemon juice	1 Tbs	1 Tbs

Bourride is one of the great fish soups of Southern France, and is a nourishing, warming meal in itself.

Cut the fish fillets into about 7½cm/3in pieces. Put the trimmings and heads into a large saucepan with all the remaining soup ingredients, except the bread and aioli, and bring to the boil. Half-cover the pan and simmer for 30 minutes.

Meanwhile, make the aioli. Soak the breadcrumbs in vinegar for 5 minutes, then squeeze dry. Transfer the crumbs to a bowl and mash in the garlic. Beat in the egg yolks, one at a time, then the salt, mustard and pepper. When the mixture is very thick and smooth, beat in the olive oil, a few drops at a time. Do not add the oil too quickly or the mayonnaise will curdle. When the mayonnaise has thickened, the oil may be added a little more rapidly. When all the oil has been added, beat in the lemon juice. Set aside.

Strain the fish stock, pressing down on the vegetables with the back of a wooden spoon. Rinse out the pan, then return the fish stock to it. Add the fish and bring to the boil. Reduce the heat to low and simmer for 10 minutes, or until the flesh flakes easily. Using a slotted spoon, transfer the fish pieces to a warmed serving bowl. Boil the stock rapidly for 10 minutes or until it has reduced a little.

Very gradually beat about 125ml/4floz (½ cup) of the fish stock into the aioli. Pour the mixture into the saucepan and simmer gently for 1 to 2 minutes, being careful not to let it curdle.

Arrange the toasted bread rounds on the bottom of individual bowls, and cover with fish pieces. Pour over the aioli stock and serve at once.

8 Servings

PATE DE FOIE
(Liver Pâté)

	Metric/U.K.	U.S.
Streaky (fatty) bacon	225g/8oz	8oz
Butter	25g/1oz	2 Tbs
Chicken livers, trimmed	225g/8oz	8oz
Minced (ground) veal	½kg/1lb	1lb
Minced (ground) pork	225g/8oz	8oz
Garlic cloves, crushed	2	2
Juniper berries, coarsely crushed	12	12
Black peppercorns, coarsely crushed	12	12
Salt and pepper to taste		
Mixed spice or allspice	¼ tsp	¼ tsp
Dry white wine	175ml/6floz	¾ cup
Dry sherry	50ml/2floz	¼ cup

Preheat the oven to moderate 180°C (Gas Mark 4, 350°F).

Dice half the bacon and put it into a mixing bowl. Reserve the remaining slices.

Melt the butter in a small frying-pan. Add the chicken livers and fry until they are well browned on the outside but pink on the inside. Transfer the livers to a chopping board. Chop them finely and transfer them to the bowl with the bacon. Add all the remaining ingredients and beat well to mix.

Turn the mixture into a well-greased medium terrine or ovenproof dish. Pack down well and cover the top with the reserved slices of bacon. Cover tightly with foil and a lid. Put the terrine into a roasting pan and pour in enough boiling water to come about two-thirds up the sides of the terrine. Place the pan in the oven and bake for 2 hours.

Remove from the oven and transfer the terrine to a board. Remove the lid and place a weight on top of the pâté. Leave to cool. When the pâté is cool, remove the weight and chill in the refrigerator for 4 hours.

Before serving, unmould on to a serving plate and cut into slices.

8 Servings

ESCARGOTS A LA BOURGUIGNONNE
(Snails with Garlic Butter)

	Metric/U.K.	U.S.
Butter, softened	175g/6oz	12 Tbs
Finely chopped parsley	2 Tbs	2 Tbs
Garlic cloves, crushed	2	2
Salt and pepper to taste		
Brandy	2 Tbs	2 Tbs
Snail shells	24	24
Canned snails, drained or frozen snails	24	24

Preheat the oven to fairly hot 190°C (Gas Mark 5, 375°F).

Cream the butter, parsley, garlic and seasoning together. Add half the brandy and beat until the mixture is soft and smooth.

Using a teaspoon, push a little of the butter mixture into each snail shell. Then push a snail into each shell and seal the entrance with a little more of the butter mixture.

Put the snails into a shallow ovenproof dish and dribble over the remaining brandy. Put the dish into the oven and bake for 15 to 20 minutes, or until the butter is bubbling and beginning to brown. Serve at once.

4 Servings

RILLETTES DE PORC
(Potted Pork)

This is the speciality of the city of Tours in the Loire valley, although versions of it are found all over France.

	Metric/U.K.	U.S.
Pork fat, cut into pieces	700g/1½lb	1½lb
Lean pork belly, cut into 5cm/2in pieces	1kg/2lb	2lb
Water	50ml/2floz	¼ cup
Salt and pepper to taste		
Dried sage	1 tsp	1 tsp
Bouquets garnis	2	2
Dried marjoram	½ tsp	½ tsp
Garlic clove, crushed	1	1

Put the pork fat, belly and water into a large saucepan and bring to the boil. Season generously with salt and pepper and add the sage and bouquets garnis. Cover and simmer the mixture for 4½ hours, checking occasionally to make sure the mixture does not become too dry (add more boiling water if this happens). Remove from the heat and remove the bouquets garnis.

Pour the mixture into a fine strainer and allow the fat to drip through into a bowl. Beat the marjoram, garlic and seasoning to taste into the mixture in the strainer, then shred with a fork. Turn the pork into small stoneware pots (or a terrine if you prefer). Pour a little of the pork fat over the top and set aside to cool completely. Cover with lids or foil and chill in the refrigerator. Use as required.

About 700g/1½lb

SALADE DE TOMATES
(Tomato Salad)

Despite the name, this is one of the most popular hors d'oeuvre dishes in the French cooking repertoire. Obviously the dressing varies from cook to cook, and if you prefer yours to be non-garlic, then the one suggested below can be amended and changed accordingly.

	Metric/U.K.	U.S.
Tomatoes, thinly sliced	450g/1lb	1lb
Chives, chopped	2 Tbs	2 Tbs
Chopped fresh basil	1 Tbs	1 Tbs
DRESSING		
Olive oil	50ml/2floz	4 Tbs
Wine vinegar	2 Tbs	2 Tbs
Garlic clove, crushed	1	1
Salt and pepper to taste		
French mustard	1 tsp	1 tsp

First make the dressing. Put all the ingredients into a screw-top jar and shake vigorously to blend.

Arrange the tomato slices, slightly overlapping, in a serving dish. Pour over the dressing, then sprinkle with chives and basil.

Chill in the refrigerator for 15 minutes before serving.

4 Servings

Snails are a particular French weakness, and a taste sometimes not quite understood outside the country. Escargots à la Bourguignonne (snails with a delicious garlic butter) will help change that opinion!

Fish and Seafood

MAQUERAUX A LA SAUCE MOUTARDE
(Mackerel Fillets in Mustard Sauce)

Basic French cooking is about doing simply delicious things with simple, plain food and this Maqueraux à la Sauce Moutarde (mackerel fillets with a piquant mustard sauce) is an excellent example.

	Metric/U.K.	U.S.
Olive oil	1 Tbs	1 Tbs
Large mackerel, cleaned	2	2
Lemon juice	1 Tbs	1 Tbs
Butter	75g/3oz	6 Tbs
French mustard	1½ Tbs	1½ Tbs
Egg yolks	2	2
Cider vinegar	1 Tbs	1 Tbs
Salt and pepper to taste		
Chopped fresh herbs (a mixture of chives, thyme, sage and marjoram)	2 Tbs	2 Tbs

Preheat the oven to moderate 180°C (Gas Mark 4, 350°F).

Grease two large pieces of aluminium foil with the oil. Lay one mackerel on each piece of foil and sprinkle over the lemon juice. Wrap the fish loosely in the foil, envelope fashion, so that it is completely enclosed, but allowing it some room to 'breathe'. Place the fish parcels in the oven and bake for 20 minutes, or until the fish flesh flakes easily.

Meanwhile, prepare the sauce. Cream the butter with a wooden spoon until it is soft and set aside.

Beat the mustard, egg yolks, vinegar and seasoning together until they are well blended. Gradually add the egg yolk mixture to the butter, beating until they are combined and the sauce is smooth and thick. Stir in the herbs. Spoon the sauce into a sauceboat and chill in the refrigerator.

Remove the mackerel parcels from the oven and open carefully. Pour the cooking juices into a bowl and reserve.

Remove the skin from the mackerel by scraping it off with the point of a knife, being careful not to break the flesh. Cut each fish into four fillets and remove the bones. Arrange the fillets on a shallow serving dish. Strain the reserved cooking juices over the fillets and allow to cool to room temperature. Chill in the refrigerator for 2 hours.

Serve cold, accompanied by the mustard sauce.

4 Servings

ROUGETS A LA NICOISE
(Red Mullets in Tomato Sauce)

Red mullets are one of the most popular of the southern French fish and are cooked in a variety of ways. This recipe assumes that the fish are medium in size, but if you can only obtain small ones, allow two per person.

	Metric/U.K.	U.S.
Olive oil	50ml/2floz	¼ cup
Tomatoes, blanched, peeled, seeded and coarsely chopped	700g/1½lb	1½lb
Garlic cloves, crushed	4	4

	Metric/U.K.	U.S.
Dried thyme	1 tsp	1 tsp
Bay leaf	1	1
Salt and pepper to taste		
Black olives, stoned (pitted)	225g/8oz	2 cups
Lemons, cut into 12 slices	2	2
Red mullets, cleaned and scaled but with the heads and tails left on	6	6

Heat the oil in a large frying-pan. Add the tomatoes, garlic, herbs and seasoning, reduce the heat to low and simmer, stirring occasionally, for 15 to 20 minutes, or until the mixture is very thick.

Stir in the olives and lemon slices, then transfer half the mixture to a second frying-pan. Divide the fish between the pans and baste them with the sauce until they are well coated.

Cover and cook, turning the fish occasionally, for 15 to 20 minutes, or until the flesh flakes easily.

Remove the bay leaf and serve at once.

6 Servings

DARNE DE SAUMON FLORENTINE
(Salmon Steaks with Spinach)

	Metric/U.K.	U.S.
Salmon steaks, cut 2½cm/1in thick	4	4
Unsalted butter, melted	50g/2oz	4 Tbs
Spinach, cooked, drained and kept hot	1½kg/3lb	3lb
Double (heavy) cream	50ml/2floz	¼ cup
Salt and pepper to taste		
SAUCE		
Unsalted butter, melted	175g/6oz	12 Tbs
Lemon juice	1 Tbs	1 Tbs

Colourful, economical and filling—Rougets à la Niçoise.

	Metric/U.K.	U.S.
Salt and white pepper to taste		
Cayenne pepper	⅛ tsp	⅛ tsp

Preheat the grill (broiler) to moderate. Arrange the steaks on the lined rack of the grill (broiler) pan. Coat them with a little of the melted butter. Grill (broil) the fish for 8 to 10 minutes on each side, basting frequently with the remaining butter, or until the flesh flakes easily.

Meanwhile, combine the spinach, cream and seasoning in a bowl. Arrange the mixture over the bottom of a large, warmed serving dish. Transfer the fish steaks to the dish and arrange them over the spinach.

Combine all the sauce ingredients together in a jug and pour over the steaks. Serve at once.

4 Servings

ROULADE DE SAUMON
(Salmon Roll)

This delicious dish is usually served with sour cream. Use fresh herbs if at all possible; if you are using dried, halve the amounts indicated below. If you aren't lucky enough to have fresh salmon handy, frozen or good-quality canned can be substituted although the taste won't be quite as good.

	Metric/U.K.	U.S.
Cooked fresh salmon, skinned	275g/10oz	10oz
Eggs, separated	4	4
Butter, melted	25g/1oz	2 Tbs
Flour	3 Tbs	3 Tbs
Salt and pepper to taste		
Chopped chives	2 tsp	2 tsp
Chopped fresh fennel	1 tsp	1 tsp
Chopped fresh marjoram	½ tsp	½ tsp
White wine vinegar	2 tsp	2 tsp
Double (heavy) cream	2 Tbs	2 Tbs

Line the base and sides of an 18cm/7in x 25cm/10in baking pan with greaseproof or waxed paper, allowing the paper to stand about 2½cm/1in above the sides of the pan. Grease the paper and set aside. Preheat the oven to moderate 180°C (Gas Mark 4, 350°F).

Purée the salmon in a blender or food mill and set aside.

Put the egg yolks in a large bowl and beat until they are pale and thick. Gradually beat in the melted butter, then stir in the flour, a tablespoon at a time, until the ingredients are thoroughly combined. Stir in the puréed salmon, seasoning, herbs, vinegar and cream until the mixture is smooth.

Beat the egg whites in a second bowl until they form stiff peaks. Carefully fold the egg whites into the salmon mixture until they are thoroughly combined.

Pour the salmon mixture into the pan and smooth the top. Put the pan into the oven and bake for 15 minutes, or until the mixture is just firm to the touch and pale golden brown. Remove from the oven. Turn the mixture out on to a large piece of greaseproof or waxed paper, then remove and discard the paper from the mixture.

Using the greaseproof or waxed paper, roll up the mixture Swiss (jelly) roll style. Transfer to a warmed serving plate and serve at once.

3-4 Servings

SOLE NORMANDE
(Sole Fillets Garnished with Mussels and Shrimps)

This is one of the great regional classics of French cuisine.

	Metric/U.K.	U.S.
Sole fillets, skinned	8	8
Mussels, scrubbed, steamed for 6-8 minutes or until they open, cooking liquid reserved	600ml/1 pint	1¼ pints
Onion, thinly sliced into rings	1	1
Bouquet garni	1	1
Dry white wine	300ml/10floz	1¼ cups
Butter	25g/1oz	2 Tbs
Shallots, halved	4	4
Button mushrooms, stalks removed	225g/8oz	2 cups
Lemon juice	1 Tbs	1 Tbs
Salt and pepper to taste		
Frozen shrimps, thawed	125g/4oz	4oz

The exquisite simplicity and richness of salmon is demonstrated in two very different but delicious dishes: on top Roulade de Saumon, below Darnes de Saumon Florentine.

The most elegant yet easy to make of fish dishes, Sole Meunière.

SAUCE		
Butter	1 Tbs	1 Tbs
Flour	2 Tbs	2 Tbs
Salt and pepper to taste		
Double (heavy) cream	250ml/8floz	1 cup

Roll up the fillets Swiss (jelly) roll style and secure with thread. Arrange the rolls in a large ovenproof dish and set aside.

Strain the reserved mussel liquid into a large saucepan. Add the onion and bouquet garni then pour over the wine. Bring the liquid to the boil. Reduce the heat to moderately low and simmer the stock for 10 minutes. Strain the stock into a large bowl and set aside.

Preheat the oven to moderate 180°C (Gas Mark 4, 350°F).

Melt the butter in a large frying-pan. Add the shallots, mushrooms, lemon juice and seasoning and fry for 5 minutes. Transfer the mixture to the dish containing the fish. Set the pan aside.

Add the mussels and shrimps to the dish and pour over the reserved stock. Put the dish into the oven and cook for 15 to 20 minutes, or until the fish flesh flakes easily. Transfer the fish rolls to a warmed serving dish. Remove and discard the thread. Transfer the shallots, mushrooms, mussels and shrimps to the serving dish and arrange decoratively around the fish. Set aside and keep hot while you make the sauce.

Strain the cooking liquid and set aside. Add the butter to the butter remaining in the frying-pan and melt it over moderate heat. Remove from the heat and, using a wooden spoon, stir in the flour to form a smooth paste. Gradually stir in the reserved cooking liquid and seasoning and return to the heat. Cook the sauce, stirring constantly, for 2 to 3 minutes, or until it is smooth and thick. Remove from the heat and stir in the cream.

Pour the sauce over the fish and serve at once.

4 Servings

SOLE MEUNIERE
(Sole Fillets with Butter Sauce)

	Metric/U.K.	U.S.
Sole fillets, skinned	700g/1½lb	1½lb
Lemon juice	3 Tbs	3 Tbs
Seasoned flour (flour with salt and pepper to taste)	50g/2oz	½ cup
Butter	125g/4oz	8 Tbs
Large lemon, thinly sliced	1	1
Parsley sprigs	6	6

Sprinkle the fillets with 2 tablespoons of the lemon juice and set aside for 5 minutes. Pat dry with kitchen towels. Dip the fillets in the seasoned flour, shaking off any excess.

Melt 75g/3oz (6 tablespoons) of the butter in a large frying-pan. Add the fillets, a few at a time, and cook them for 4 to 6 minutes on each side, or until the flesh flakes easily. Arrange the fillets in a warmed, shallow serving dish.

Wipe the pan clean and add the remaining juice and butter. Place over low heat and simmer until the butter melts, stirring constantly.

Remove from the heat and pour the butter over the fillets. Garnish with lemon slices and parsley.

Serve at once.

6 Servings

TRUITES AUX AMANDES
(Trout with Almonds)

	Metric/U.K.	U.S.
Medium trout, cleaned and with the eyes removed	6	6
Salt and white pepper to taste		
Lemon juice	2 Tbs	2 Tbs
Milk	175ml/6floz	¾ cup
Seasoned flour (flour with salt and pepper to taste)	75g/3oz	¾ cup
Butter	150g/5oz	10 Tbs
Slivered almonds	125g/4oz	1 cup
Lemon quarters	6	6

Gently rub the fish with the seasoning and half the lemon juice.

Dip the fish first in the milk, then in the seasoned flour, shaking off any excess.

Melt 75g/3oz (6 tablespoons) of the butter in a large frying-pan. Add the trout and fry for 4 to 6 minutes on each side, or until the flesh flakes easily. Transfer the fish to a warmed serving dish. Keep warm.

Add the remaining butter in the pan. Stir in the almonds and remaining lemon juice and fry until the almonds are golden brown.

Pour the mixture over the trout and garnish with the lemon quarters. Serve at once.

6 Servings

HARENGS A LA BOULANGERE
(Herrings Baked with Potatoes and Onions)

French cooking isn't just elegant sauces and expensive ingredients, it's also combining the everyday and inexpensive, and making of them something very special. This herring dish is baked with the classic boulangère garnish of potatoes and onions and the result is superb—and cheap and easy to make.

	Metric/U.K.	U.S.
Medium potatoes, parboiled for 5 minutes, then thinly sliced	4	4
Herrings, filleted and cleaned	6	6
Dried marjoram	½ tsp	½ tsp
Dried thyme	½ tsp	½ tsp
Salt and pepper to taste		
Lemon juice	1 Tbs	1 Tbs
Medium onions, thinly sliced into rings	2	2
Water	125ml/4floz	½ cup
Butter	25g/1oz	2 Tbs

Preheat the oven to fairly hot 190°C (Gas Mark 5, 375°F).

Line the bottom of a large, well-greased baking dish with half the potato slices. Lay the fillets on top and sprinkle over the herbs and seasoning. Pour over the lemon juice and cover with onion slices. Lay the remaining potato slices on top. Pour over the water. Cut the butter into small pieces and dot them on top of the potatoes, and season to taste.

Cover the dish and put into the oven. Bake for 40 minutes, or until the potatoes are cooked through and the fish flesh flakes easily.

Serve immediately, from the dish.

4-6 Servings

MOULES MARINIERE
(Mussels in White Wine)

This is one of the most popular of French fish dishes and is a specialty of Brittany. It should be eaten in large bowls, rather like soup—with an extra bowl for the shells.

	Metric/U.K.	U.S.
Shallots, finely chopped	2	2
Garlic clove, crushed	1	1
Bouquet garni	1	1
Parsley sprigs	2	2
Mussels, scrubbed, soaked for 1 hour in cold water and drained	3l/6 pints	3½ qts
Dry white wine	600ml/1 pint	2½ cups
Butter, cut into small pieces	50g/2oz	4 Tbs
Salt and pepper to taste		
Chopped parsley	2 Tbs	2 Tbs

Put the shallots, garlic and herbs in a large buttered saucepan.

Discard any mussels which are not tightly shut or do not close if sharply tapped, and any that have broken shells or have floated in the water. Arrange the remaining mussels in the pan and pour over the wine. Scatter over half the butter, cover and bring to the boil. Cook for 6 to 8 minutes, or until the mussel shells open. Remove the mussels from the pan and remove one shell from each one. Arrange the mussels in a warmed serving dish and keep hot.

Remove the bouquet garni and parsley sprigs from the pan and boil the liquid rapidly until it has reduced by one-third and has thickened. Stir in the seasoning and remaining butter until it has melted.

Pour over the mussels, sprinkle over the

Huitres Marinées, a delicious new way with oysters.

parsley and serve at once.

4 Servings

HUITRES MARINEES
(Marinated Oysters)

There are two main areas of oyster production in France, at Marennes off the coast of Bordeaux, and around the coasts of Brittany. This dish, with regional embellishments is popular in both areas, and is eaten as an hors d'oeuvre or (in double quantities and by afficionados) as a light lunch. The traditional wine to serve with an oyster dish such as this, by the way, is chilled Chablis.

	Metric/U.K.	U.S.
Oysters	16	16
MARINADE		
Dry white wine	175ml/6floz	¾ cup
Olive oil	50ml/2floz	¼ cup
Lemon juice	50ml/2floz	¼ cup
Salt and pepper to taste		
Dried thyme	¼ tsp	¼ tsp
Dried chervil	¼ tsp	¼ tsp
Chopped parsley	1 tsp	1 tsp
Garlic clove, crushed	1	1

First, prepare the marinade. Combine all the ingredients in a large bowl, stirring to blend thoroughly. Set aside for 15 minutes.

Meanwhile, detach the oysters from the shells and put them into a saucepan. Discard the shells. Add the marinade and bring the liquid to the boil.

Transfer the oysters and liquid to a serving bowl and set aside to cool to room temperature. Chill in the refrigerator until required. Serve cold, in the marinade.

2-4 Servings

COQUILLES SAINT-JACQUES A L'AIL
(Scallops with Garlic and Basil)

	Metric/U.K.	U.S.
Scallops, cut into 1cm/½in pieces	700g/1½lb	1½lb
Lemon juice	1 Tbs	1 Tbs
Salt and white pepper to taste		
Seasoned flour (flour with salt and pepper to taste)	50g/2oz	½ cup
Vegetable oil	75ml/3floz	6 Tbs
Shallots, finely chopped	3	3
Garlic cloves, crushed	3	3
Dried basil	¼ tsp	¼ tsp
Butter	25g/1oz	2 Tbs
Chopped parsley	1 Tbs	1 Tbs

A classic dish of scallops, Coquilles Saint-Jacques à l'Ail.

Dry the scallops on kitchen towels and place them on a piece of greaseproof or waxed paper. Sprinkle over the lemon juice, salt and pepper. Set aside for 5 minutes. Dip the scallops in the flour, shaking off any excess.

Heat the oil in a large frying-pan. Add the scallops and fry for 5 minutes, turning occasionally, or until they are lightly browned. Stir in the shallots, garlic and basil and cook for a further 2 minutes. Remove from the heat and stir in the butter and parsley.

Transfer to a warmed serving dish or individual scallop shells and serve at once.

4 Servings

Alouettes Sans Têtes is the rather gory name for this superb dish of stuffed beef rolls.

Meat

ALOUETTES SANS TETES
(Stuffed Beef Rolls)

Despite its bizarre name (it means, literally, larks without heads) this dish is really stuffed beef rolls, or paupiettes as they are sometimes called in France. Because of the long slow cooking time, an inexpensive cut of meat can be used, braising or chuck steak, for instance, as well as the more usual paupiette beef topside (top rump).

	Metric/U.K.	U.S.
Lean beef, cut 12½cm/5in square by ½cm/¼in thick	8 slices	8 slices
Vegetable oil	2 Tbs	2 Tbs
Onions, chopped	2	2
Carrots, chopped	2	2
Beef stock	300ml/10floz	1¼ cups
Tomatoes, blanched, peeled, seeded and chopped	3	3
Garlic clove, crushed	1	1
Bay leaf	1	1
Chopped parsley	2 Tbs	2 Tbs
STUFFING		
Minced (ground) pork or veal	175g/6oz	6oz
Small onion, finely chopped	1	1
Butter, softened	25g/1oz	2 Tbs
Fresh white breadcrumbs	25g/1oz	½ cup
Finely chopped parsley	1 Tbs	1 Tbs
Dried sage	1 tsp	1 tsp
Finely grated lemon rind	1½ tsp	1½ tsp
Egg, lightly beaten	1	1
Salt and pepper to taste		

Preheat the oven to moderate 180°C (Gas Mark 4, 350°F).

To prepare the stuffing, mix all the ingredients together until they are thoroughly blended.

Lay the beef slices out flat on a working surface and divide the stuffing among them, spreading it out carefully. Roll up the slices, Swiss (jelly) roll style and tie with string or thread.

Heat the oil in a large saucepan. Add the rolls and fry, turning frequently, until they are evenly browned. Transfer them to a large casserole.

Add the onions and carrots to the pan and fry until they are soft. Stir in the stock, tomatoes, garlic and bay leaf and bring to the boil. Pour the mixture over the beef rolls and cover the casserole tightly. Put the dish into the oven and cook for 1½ hours, or until the rolls are cooked through and tender.

Transfer the beef rolls to a warmed serving dish and remove the string or thread. Keep hot. Strain the cooking liquid into a jug or pan, pressing down on the vegetables and flavourings with the back of a wooden spoon. Bring to the boil and adjust the seasonings if necessary.

Pour the sauce over the beef rolls, sprinkle over the parsley and serve at once.

4 Servings

FONDUE BOURGUIGNONNE
(Beef Fondue with Sauces)

Fondue is traditionally Swiss, but the French have adapted the original cheese idea and applied it to meat—and the result is as below. The beef is speared on special fondue forks and placed in the boiling oil until cooked to taste. The dips and sauces suggested here are just that, suggestions— any sauce or garnish may be used so long as it complements the meat.

	Metric/U.K.	U.S.
Medium onion, finely chopped	1	1
Large dessert apple, cored, finely chopped and sprinkled with a little tarragon vinegar	1	1
Large pickled gherkins, finely chopped	2	2
Capers, finely chopped	1 Tbs	1 Tbs
Chopped fresh herbs (chives, basil, parsley or chervil)	1 Tbs	1 Tbs
French mustard	4 Tbs	4 Tbs
Prepared horseradish sauce or relish	4 Tbs	4 Tbs
Aioli sauce or mayonnaise	125ml/4floz	½ cup
Fillet or rump steak	1kg/2lb	2lb
Vegetable oil	600ml/1 pint	2½ cups
TOMATO SAUCE Butter	25g/1oz	2 Tbs
Tomatoes, blanched, peeled and halved	3	3
Dried basil	1 tsp	1 tsp
Salt and pepper to taste		
Tomato purée (paste)	2 tsp	2 tsp

First make the tomato sauce. Melt the butter in a small saucepan. Add the tomatoes, basil and seasoning and simmer for 10 minutes, stirring occasionally, or until the tomatoes have pulped. Strain into a bowl, rubbing the tomatoes through with the back of a wooden spoon. Stir in the tomato purée (paste). Allow the mixture to cool completely, then transfer to a shallow serving dish. Set aside.

Put the onion, apple, gherkins, capers, herbs, mustard, horseradish and aioli or mayonnaise in small individual serving dishes.

Cut the beef into 2½cm/1in cubes and arrange them on a large serving dish.

Heat the oil in a saucepan until it reaches 190°C (375°F) on a deep-fat thermometer, or until a small cube of stale bread dropped into the oil turns golden brown in 40 seconds. Carefully pour the oil into a fondue pot.

Light the spirit burner and place the fondue pot over it. The oil is now ready for cooking the steak.

6 Servings

BOEUF BOURGUIGNON
(Beef Stew with Red Wine)

This dish, not surprisingly given its name, originated in the province of Burgundy where they produce a lot of wine and can afford to use large amounts of it in cooking! Its popularity,

however, has long since spread beyond its native province and it is now one of the two or three best-known examples of French cuisine both inside and outside France.

	Metric/U.K.	U.S.
Streaky (fatty) bacon, cut into strips	175g/6oz	6oz
Olive oil	1 Tbs	1 Tbs
Chuck or braising steak, cubed	1½kg/3lb	3lb
Carrot, sliced	1	1
Onion, sliced	1	1
Salt and pepper to taste		
Flour	25g/1oz	4 Tbs
Red wine	750ml/1¼ pts	3 cups
Beef stock	450ml/15floz	2 cups
Garlic cloves, crushed	3	3
Dried thyme	½ tsp	½ tsp
Bay leaf	1	1
Chopped parsley	2 Tbs	2 Tbs
VEGETABLES Butter	50g/2oz	4 Tbs
Vegetable oil	1½ Tbs	1½ Tbs
Small pickling or pearl onions	18	18
Beef stock or red wine	150ml/5floz	⅝ cup
Bouquet garni	1	1
Salt and pepper to taste		
Mushrooms, quartered	½kg/1lb	4 cups

Blanch the bacon strips in boiling water for 5 minutes, then dry on kitchen towels. Set aside.

Heat the oil in a large flameproof casserole. Add the bacon and fry until the strips are evenly browned. Transfer the strips to a plate.

Reheat the fat until it is very hot. Add the beef cubes and fry until they are evenly browned. Transfer the cubes to the plate with the bacon. Add the carrot and onion to the casserole and fry until they are soft. Pour off the fat from the casserole and return the beef and bacon to it. Season to taste, sprinkle over the flour and toss lightly with a wooden spoon.

Preheat the oven to warm 170°C (Gas Mark 3, 325°F).

Stir the wine, stock, garlic and herbs into the casserole and bring to the boil. Cover and put the casserole into the oven. Cook for 3½ to 4 hours, or until the meat is very tender.

Meanwhile, prepare the vegetables. Melt half the butter and half the oil in a frying-pan. Add the onions and fry until they are evenly browned. Pour in the stock or wine, bouquet garni and seasoning. Cover and simmer for 40 minutes, or until they are tender but still firm. Transfer to a plate. Discard the juices in the pan.

Add the remaining butter and oil to the pan. Add the mushrooms and fry for 5 minutes, or until they are cooked. Transfer to the onions.

Arrange the meat, onions and mushrooms on a serving dish and keep hot. Strain the casserole juice into a saucepan and boil rapidly until it has reduced and thickened. Pour over the meat and vegetables, and serve at once.

6-8 Servings

DAUBE DE BOEUF A LA PROVENCALE
(Beef Stew with Tomatoes, Mushrooms and Olives)

Daubes are a type of marinated beef stew found all over the southern part of France. They are quite economical to cook since marination tenderizes meat, which means that the cheapest type of stewing steak may be used. This is a local variation on the theme from Provence.

	Metric/U.K.	U.S.
Lean stewing steak, cubed	1½kg/3lb	3lb
Streaky (fatty) bacon, cut into strips	225g/8oz	8oz
Flour	125g/4oz	1 cup
Mushrooms, sliced	225g/8oz	2 cups
Tomatoes, blanched, peeled, seeded and chopped	700g/1½lb	1½lb
Garlic cloves, crushed	3	3
Grated orange rind	1 tsp	1 tsp
Chopped parsley	1 Tbs	1 Tbs
Bouquet garni	1	1
Beef stock	175ml/6floz	¾ cup
Black olives, stoned (pitted) and halved	12	12
MARINADE Dry white wine	300ml/10floz	1¼ cups

Daubes are a type of marinated stew very popular all over France but traditional to the southern part. Daube de Boeuf la Provençale is a superb variation on the theme.

	Metric/U.K.	U.S.
Brandy	50ml/2floz	$\frac{1}{4}$ cup
Salt	2 tsp	2 tsp
Black peppercorns	1 tsp	1 tsp
Dried thyme	$\frac{1}{2}$ tsp	$\frac{1}{2}$ tsp
Bay leaf	1	1
Garlic cloves, crushed	2	2
Medium onions, thinly sliced	4	4
Medium carrots, sliced	4	4

Combine all the marinade ingredients in a large bowl and add the beef cubes. Set aside at room temperature for at least 8 hours (or overnight in the refrigerator), basting occasionally.

Blanch the bacon strips in boiling water for 5 minutes then dry on kitchen towels. Set aside.

Remove the beef cubes from the marinade and pat dry on kitchen towels. Strain the marinade into a bowl, reserving both liquid and vegetables. Discard the bay leaf.

Preheat the oven to warm 170°C (Gas Mark 3, 325°F).

Dip the beef cubes in the flour, shaking off any excess.

Arrange two or three bacon strips over the bottom of a large flameproof casserole. Spoon over a few of the marinated vegetables, then mushrooms and tomatoes. Arrange a layer of beef over the vegetables, and sprinkle with crushed garlic, orange rind and parsley. Add the bouquet garni. Continue making layers as before, ending with a layer of bacon. Pour over the beef stock and reserved marinade liquid, and scatter over the olives. Bring the liquid to the boil, then transfer to the oven. Braise for 4 hours, or until the meat is very tender.

Remove from the oven and skim any fat from the surface. Adjust the seasoning, discard the bouquet garni and serve at once.

6-8 Servings

ENTRECOTES AU POIVRE
(Steaks with Crushed Peppercorns)

	Metric/U.K.	U.S.
Black peppercorns	3 Tbs	3 Tbs
Butter	50g/2oz	4 Tbs
Entrecôte steaks, about 175g/6oz each	4	4
Brandy	2 Tbs	2 Tbs
Double (heavy) cream	150ml/5floz	$\frac{5}{8}$ cup

Put the peppercorns into a mortar and crush them coarsely with a pestle. Transfer them to a plate. Press the steaks into the crushed peppercorns, coating both sides and shaking off any excess.

Melt the butter in a large frying-pan. Add the steaks and fry for 2 minutes on each side over moderately high heat. Reduce the heat to moderately low and fry for a further 3 minutes on each side. This will give you rare steaks; double the cooking time for well-done steaks. Transfer the steaks to a large, warmed serving platter. Keep hot.

Add the brandy to the pan and stir well. Stir in the cream and cook for 3 minutes, stirring and scraping the bottom of the pan. Pour over the steaks and serve at once.

4 Servings

BOEUF EN CROUTE
(Fillet of Beef in Pastry, Called Beef Wellington)

This is one of the most spectacular dishes in all of haute cuisine *and although it takes a little care in preparation, the end result is more than worth the effort.*

	Metric/U.K.	U.S.
Puff pastry dough	575g/1¼lb	1¼lb
FILLING		
Fillet or côntrefilet of beef, with excess fat removed	1x1½kg/3lb	1x3lb
Brandy	1 Tbs	1 Tbs
Salt and pepper to taste		
Streaky (fatty) bacon	6 slices	6 slices
Pâté de foie gras	225g/8oz	8oz
Egg, lightly beaten	1	1
SAUCE		
Butter	75g/3oz	6 Tbs
Shallots, finely chopped	6	6
Beef stock	600ml/1 pint	2½ cups
Madeira	225ml/7floz	$\frac{7}{8}$ cup

Preheat the oven to very hot 230°F (Gas Mark 8, 450°F).

Rub the fillet all over with the brandy and

season with salt and pepper. Cover the top with the bacon slices and put the meat in the rack in a roasting pan. Put the pan into the oven and roast the meat for 20 minutes, if you want the meat to be rare, and 10 minutes longer if you prefer medium meat. Remove the pan from the oven and remove the meat from the pan. Discard the bacon and set the meat aside to cool to room temperature. When the meat has cooled, spread the pâté over the top and sides.

Reduce the oven temperature to hot 220°C (Gas Mark 7, 425°F).

Roll out the pastry dough to a rectangle about 45cm/18in x 30cm/12in by $\frac{1}{2}$cm/$\frac{1}{4}$in thick. Put the meat on the dough, top side down, with the long sides of the meat parallel to the long sides of the dough. Wrap the meat in the dough to make a neat parcel, trimming off any excess. Brush the joins with a little beaten egg and crimp to seal. Be careful not to wrap the meat too tightly because the pastry will shrink slightly during cooking.

Arrange the meat on a baking sheet, seam side down. Mark a criss-cross pattern on the top, then brush the top and sides with a little more beaten egg. Roll out the dough trimmings and use them to decorate the top of the parcel.

Put the sheet into the oven and bake the meat for 30 minutes, or until the pastry is golden brown.

Meanwhile, to make the sauce, melt a third of the butter in a saucepan. Add the shallots and fry until they are golden brown. Pour over the stock and 150ml/5floz ($\frac{5}{8}$ cup) of Madeira. Bring to the boil and boil for 30 minutes or until the liquid has reduced by about half. Strain the sauce into a bowl, then return to the saucepan and bring to the boil. Remove from the heat and stir in the remaining butter until it has melted, then the remaining Madeira. Transfer the sauce to a warmed sauceboat. Keep hot.

When the meat has finished cooking, turn off the oven and leave the meat in the oven for 15 minutes.

Remove and serve carved into thin slices. Accompany the meat with the sauce.

8-12 Servings

One of the most elegant and famous of haute cuisine *dishes, Boeuf en Croûte is equally popular outside France, where it is sometimes called Beef Wellington.*

NAVARIN PRINTANIER
(Mutton Stew with Vegetables)

The secret of this French classic is in the vegetables—to be really authentic, fresh young spring vegetables should be used. If mutton is difficult to obtain, lamb may be substituted but needs to cook for only an hour to an hour and a quarter altogether.

Noisettes are small, succulent lamb chops with the bones removed, and they are a feature of haute cuisine. In Noisettes d' Agneau à la Clamart, they are served over small pastry cases filled with fresh, puréed garden peas.

	Metric/U.K.	U.S.
Salt pork, diced	125g/4oz	4oz
Boned breast of mutton, trimmed of excess fat and cubed	700g/1½lb	1½lb
Boned shoulder of mutton, trimmed of excess fat and cubed	700g/1½lb	1½lb
Soft brown sugar	2 Tbs	2 Tbs
Salt and pepper to taste		
Flour	½ Tbs	½ Tbs
Medium tomatoes, blanched, peeled, seeded and chopped	6	6
Chicken stock	1¼l/2 pints	5 cups
Bouquet garni	1	1
Butter	50g/2oz	¼ cup
Small potatoes, peeled	12	12
Small turnips, whole	6	6
Small carrots, whole or halved	6	6

Small pickling or pearl		
onions	12	12
Sugar	½ Tbs	½ Tbs

Fry the salt pork in a large heavy-bottomed saucepan until it resembles small croûtons and has rendered most of its fat. Transfer the salt pork to a plate.

Add the meat to the pan and fry until it is lightly and evenly browned. Transfer the meat to the salt pork.

Remove the pan from the heat and pour off about half of the fat. Return the meat cubes and salt pork to the pan and sprinkle over the sugar and seasoning. Cook for 3 minutes, stirring constantly, or until the sugar has caramelized. Add the flour and cook for a further 3 minutes, stirring constantly. Stir in the tomatoes, stock and bouquet garni, and bring to the boil. Cover and simmer for 1 hour.

Meanwhile, prepare the vegetables. Melt the butter in a large frying-pan. Add the vegetables and fry until the onions are golden brown. Stir in the sugar and fry for a further 3 minutes or until it has dissolved. Remove the pan from the heat and transfer the vegetables to the saucepan containing the meat. Skim off any fat from the surface. Cook for 25 minutes, or until the meat and vegetables are cooked through and tender.

Remove from the heat and skim any fat from the surface of the stew. Discard the bouquet garni and transfer the stew to a large, warmed serving dish.

Serve at once.

6 Servings

SAUTE D'AGNEAU
(Lamb Stew)

	Metric/U.K.	U.S.
Olive oil	3 Tbs	3 Tbs
Lean stewing lamb, cubed	1kg/2lb	2lb
Celery stalk, chopped	1	1
Onion, finely chopped	1	1
Red wine	125ml/4floz	½ cup
Beef stock	250ml/8floz	1 cup
Cornflour (cornstarch), blended with 2 Tbs water	1 Tbs	1 Tbs
Tomato purée (paste)	2 Tbs	2 Tbs

Salt and pepper to taste		
Grated lemon rind	1 tsp	1 tsp
Button mushrooms, sliced	125g/4oz	1 cup

Heat 2 tablespoons of the oil in a flameproof casserole. Add the lamb cubes and fry quickly over moderately high heat until they are deeply and evenly browned. Transfer the meat to a plate and keep warm.

Reduce the heat to moderate and add the remaining oil to the casserole. Add the vegetables and fry until they are soft. Pour over the wine and stock, then stir in the cornflour (cornstarch) mixture and bring to the boil. Return the meat to the pan and stir in the remaining ingredients. Cover the casserole and cook for 15 minutes. (If you prefer your meat well done, increase the final cooking time by 10 minutes.)

Remove from the heat and serve at once.

4 Servings

NOISETTES D'AGNEAU A LA CLAMART
(Boned Lamb Chops in Pastry Cases with Puréed Peas)

	Metric/U.K.	U.S.
Shortcrust pastry	125g/4oz	4oz
Salt	1 tsp	1 tsp
Fresh peas, weighed after shelling	½kg/1lb	2 cups
Butter	40g/1½oz	3 Tbs
Lamb noisettes	8	8

Preheat the oven to fairly hot 200°C (Gas Mark 6, 400°F).

Roll out the pastry dough to a circle about ½cm/¼in thick. Using a 7½cm/3in pastry cutter, cut the dough into circles and use them to line eight well-greased patty tins. Cover with foil and weigh down with beans or rice. Put the tins into the oven and bake blind for 10 minutes. Remove from the oven and remove the beans or rice and foil. Bake the pastry cases for a further 5 minutes, or until they are cooked through and golden brown. Remove the tins from the oven and allow the tartlets to cool in the tins. Turn off the oven. Cover the tartlets with aluminium foil or waxed paper and return to the oven to keep warm while you

Cotelettes d'Agneau au Concombre—elegant enough for the most sophisticated dinner party, simple enough for a quiet supper at home.

prepare the remaining garnish.

Cook the peas in boiling, salted water for 15 to 20 minutes or until they are tender. Drain in a colander and either push them through a strainer using the back of a wooden spoon, or purée them in a blender. Transfer the purée to a saucepan and add 1 tablespoon of the butter. Place the pan over low heat and cook, stirring constantly, until the purée is smooth and hot. Remove from the heat. Remove the pastry cases from the oven and spoon equal portions of the purée into each one. Return to the oven to keep warm while you fry the noisettes.

Melt the remaining butter in a frying-pan. Add the noisettes and fry them for 4 to 6 minutes on each side, or until they are tender but still slightly pink inside. Remove the pan from the heat and transfer the noisettes to a plate.

Transfer the pastry cases to a warmed serving dish. Arrange the noisettes on top of the cases.

Serve at once.

4 Servings

COTELETTES D'AGNEAU AU CONCOMBRE
(Lamb Cutlets with Cucumber and Onion)

	Metric/U.K.	U.S.
Lamb cutlets	8	8
Seasoned flour (flour with salt and pepper to taste)	50g/2oz	½ cup
Egg, lightly beaten	1	1
Dry breadcrumbs	125g/4oz	1⅓ cups
Cucumbers, peeled and cut into chunks	1½	1½
Spring onions (scallions), with 5cm/2in of green tops	18	18
Butter	50g/2oz	4 Tbs
Salt and pepper to taste		
Chopped mint	1 tsp	1 tsp
Vegetable oil	75ml/3floz	⅜ cup
MOUSSELINE SAUCE		
Egg yolks	3	3

	Metric/U.K.	U.S.
Butter, melted	75g/3oz	6 Tbs
Lemon juice	2 Tbs	2 Tbs
Salt and pepper to taste		
Double (heavy) cream	50ml/2floz	¼ cup

To make the sauce, half-fill a saucepan with water and bring to the boil. Reduce the heat to very low. Put the egg yolks and 1 tablespoon of the butter into a heatproof bowl and set the bowl over the pan. Using a wooden spoon, gradually work the butter into the egg yolks. Continue stirring for about 5 minutes, or until the yolks begin to thicken. Stir in the lemon juice. Add the remaining butter, a tablespoon at a time, stirring well after each addition. The butter should be added very slowly. Be careful not to let the bowl become too hot or the egg yolks will curdle. When all the butter has been incorporated and the sauce is smooth and thick, remove the bowl from the pan. Stir in seasoning and cream and set aside.

Dip the cutlets first in the seasoned flour, then in the egg and finally in the breadcrumbs, shaking off any excess. Set aside.

Put the cucumbers and spring onions (scallions) in a large bowl and pour over enough boiling water to cover completely. Leave for 1 minute, then drain thoroughly.

Melt the butter in a saucepan. Add the spring onions (scallions), cucumber and seasoning. Cover and simmer the vegetables for 6 minutes, or until the cucumbers are tender. Remove from the heat and stir in the mint.

Heat the oil in a large frying-pan. Add the cutlets to the pan and fry for 3 to 5 minutes on each side or until they are cooked through.

Two minutes before the cutlets are cooked, replace the bowl with the sauce over the hot water and reheat gently, taking care not to bring to the boil. Remove from the pan and pour into a warmed sauceboat.

Arrange the cutlets on a warmed serving dish standing upright to form a crown. Pile the cucumber and spring onion (scallion) mixture in the centre and serve with the sauce.

4 Servings

CARRE DE PORC AU GUINIEVRE
(Loin of Pork with Juniper Berries)

Juniper berries are quite widely used in French cooking, especially with pork, ham and sauerkraut. Their addition to this simple dish adds a piquancy and spice to what otherwise would be somewhat bland.

Carré de Porc au Guinièvre, lean tender pork loin flavoured with juniper berries.

	Metric/U.K.	U.S.
Boned loin of pork, trimmed of excess fat	1x2kg/4lb	1x4lb
Garlic cloves, thinly sliced	2	2
Juniper berriers, coarsely crushed	12	12
Salt and pepper to taste		
Beef stock	300ml/10floz	1¼ cups
Dry white wine	150ml/5floz	⅝ cup

Preheat the oven to fairly hot 190°C (Gas Mark 5, 375°F).

Make small incisions all over the pork and insert the garlic slices. Sprinkle with the juniper berries and seasoning and roll up Swiss (jelly) roll style, securing it at 2½cm/1in intervals with string.

Put the meat on a rack in a roasting pan and put the pan into the oven. Roast for 2 to 2½ hours, or 30 to 35 minutes per half kilo (pound), depending on the thickness of the cut, or until the meat is cooked through and tender.

Remove the pan from the oven. Remove the pork from the pan. Wrap in foil and return to the turned-off oven to keep hot while you make the sauce.

Pour off the fat from the roasting pan. Scrape up any brown bits that have stuck to the bottom and sides. Add the stock and wine and bring to the boil, stirring constantly. Boil for 8 to 10 minutes, or until the liquid has reduced and thickened slightly. Pour into a warmed sauceboat.

Remove the pork from the oven and discard the foil. Arrange the pork on a warmed serving dish and serve at once, accompanied by the sauce.

8-10 Servings

COTES DE PORC CHARCUTIERE
(Pork Chops Braised in Piquant Sauce)

	Metric/U.K.	U.S.
Olive oil	50ml/2floz	¼ cup
Large pork chops	6	6
Medium onions, thinly sliced	3	3
Flour	1 Tbs	1 Tbs
Dry white wine	250ml/8floz	1 cup
Beef stock	125ml/4floz	½ cup
Tomato purée (paste)	1 Tbs	1 Tbs
Dried sage	½ tsp	½ tsp
Dried rosemary	½ tsp	½ tsp
Garlic cloves, crushed	2	2
Salt and pepper to taste		
French mustard	1½ tsp	1½ tsp
Medium gherkin, sliced	1	1
Cornflour (cornstarch), blended with 1 Tbs water (optional)	1 tsp	1 tsp
Chopped parsley	2 Tbs	2 Tbs

Preheat the oven to warm 170°C (Gas Mark 3, 325°F).

Heat the oil in a flameproof casserole. Add the chops and brown on all sides. (You may have to do this in batches.) As the chops

brown, transfer them to a heated platter.

Add the onions to the casserole, reduce the heat to low and simmer until they are soft. Stir in the flour until it has dissolved.

Pour the wine and stock into the casserole and stir in the tomato purée (paste), herbs, garlic and seasoning. Bring to the boil, cover and simmer the sauce for 5 minutes. Stir in the mustard, then return the chops to the casserole, basting them well with the sauce. Cover and put the casserole into the oven. Braise for 45 to 55 minutes, or until the chops are cooked through and tender.

Transfer the chops to a warmed serving dish. Put the casserole over the heat and bring to the boil. Cook for 2 to 3 minutes, then stir in the sliced gherkin. Taste and adjust the seasoning if necessary. (If you prefer a thicker sauce, add the cornflour [cornstarch] mixture, stirring until it has dissolved, then cook the sauce for a further 2 to 3 minutes.)

Pour the sauce over the chops, sprinkle over the parsley and serve at once.

6 Servings

TOURTE DE PORC
(Pork Pie)

	Metric/U.K.	U.S.
Puff pastry dough	350g/12oz	12oz
Egg yolk, lightly beaten	1	1
FILLING		
Lean minced (ground) pork	1kg/2lb	2lb
Brandy	50ml/2floz	¼ cup
Butter	15g/½oz	1 Tbs
Vegetable oil	2 Tbs	2 Tbs
Shallots, finely chopped	2	2
Garlic clove, crushed	1	1
Chopped fresh sage	1 Tbs	1 Tbs
Chopped parsley	1 Tbs	1 Tbs
Chopped fresh chervil	1 Tbs	1 Tbs
Salt and pepper to taste		
Cornflour (cornstarch), blended with 1 Tbs water	1 Tbs	1 Tbs

First prepare the filling. Put the pork into a large bowl and pour over the brandy. Set aside to marinate for 1 hour.

Meanwhile, melt the butter with the oil in

The French version of pork pie, Tourte de Porc. It contains a delicious mixture of minced (ground) pork, brandy and herbs.

One of the simplest yet most popular veal stews in the French cooking repertoire, Blanquette de Veau.

a large frying-pan. Add the shallots and garlic and fry until the shallots are soft. Add the pork and brandy and fry, stirring frequently, until the pork loses its pinkness. Stir in the herbs and seasoning and cook, stirring occasionally, for 15 minutes. Remove from the heat and stir in the cornflour (cornstarch) mixture.

Preheat the oven to hot 220°C (Gas Mark 7, 425°F).

Divide the dough in half and roll out one-half into a circle large enough to line a 23cm/9in pie plate. Press gently into the bottom and sides of the plate and trim off any excess. Spoon the filling into the centre, doming it up slightly.

Roll out the remaining dough in the same way and place it over the filling so that it covers it completely. Trim the edges, then crimp the edges together to seal. Cut a large cross in the centre. Roll out the trimmings and use them to decorate the top of the pie. Brush the top of the dough with the beaten egg yolk.

Put the plate into the oven and bake for 5 minutes. Reduce the heat to moderate 180°C (Gas Mark 4, 350°F) and bake for a further 30 minutes or until the pastry is golden brown. Remove from the oven and serve at once.

4-6 Servings

BLANQUETTE DE VEAU
(Veal in Cream Sauce)

	Metric/U.K.	U.S.
Stewing veal, cubed	700g/1½lb	1½lb
Medium onions, each studded with 2 cloves	2	2
Medium carrots, quartered	2	2
Bouquet garni	1	1
Salt and pepper to taste		
Butter	40g/1½oz	3 Tbs
Flour	40g/1½oz	⅓ cup
Single (light) cream	150ml/5floz	⅝ cup
Egg yolks	2	2
White bread, toasted and cut into triangles	4 slices	4 slices
Lemon slices (to garnish)		
Parsley sprigs (to garnish)		

Put the veal cubes into a saucepan and add just enough water to cover. Bring to the boil, then simmer for 2 minutes. Skim off any scum from the surface. Add the vegetables, bouquet

garni and seasoning and cover the pan. Simmer for $1\frac{1}{2}$ to 2 hours, or until the meat is cooked through and tender.

Transfer the meat and carrots to a warmed serving dish. Remove the cloves from the onions and quarter them. Add to the meat. Cover the mixture and keep hot while you make the sauce. Strain the cooking liquid into a bowl and reserve about 725ml/$1\frac{1}{4}$ pints (3 cups) for the sauce.

Melt the butter in a saucepan. Remove from the heat and stir in the flour to form a smooth paste. Gradually stir in the reserved stock. Return to the heat and bring to the boil. Cook the sauce for 2 to 3 minutes, stirring constantly, or until it is thick and smooth. Remove from the heat.

Combine the cream and egg yolks in a small bowl. Gradually stir about 4 tablespoons of the hot sauce into the mixture. Return the mixture to the saucepan, whisking it in, a little at a time, until the sauce is thoroughly blended. Replace the pan over low heat and simmer until the sauce is hot but not boiling.

Pour the sauce over the veal and garnish with the toast triangles, lemon slices and parsley sprigs. Serve at once.

4 Servings

TENDRONS DE VEAU AUX EPINARDS
(Breast of Veal with Spinach)

This inexpensive country dish utilizes two of France's favourite vegetables, spinach and sorrel. If you find it difficult to obtain fresh sorrel, use all spinach instead.

	Metric/U.K.	U.S.
Breast of veal, trimmed of excess fat and cubed	1kg/2lb	2lb
Seasoned flour (flour with salt and pepper to taste)	50g/2oz	$\frac{1}{2}$ cup
Eggs, beaten	2	2
Cheddar or Gruyère cheese, grated	125g/4oz	1 cup
Spinach, chopped	1kg/2lb	2lb
Sorrel, chopped	225g/8oz	8oz
Sufficient vegetable oil for deep-frying		

Coat the meat cubes first in the seasoned flour, then in the eggs and finally in the cheese, shaking off any excess.

Put the spinach and sorrel into a saucepan

A simple, economical veal stew with nutritious spinach, that's Tendrons de Veau aux Epinards.

and gently cook for 5 to 8 minutes, or until they are cooked and tender. (You need not add water—there will be sufficient moisture clinging to the leaves to provide enough for cooking.) Remove the pan from the heat and drain the vegetables, pressing down on them with a plate to extract all the liquid. Chop the vegetables and arrange them around the edge of a warmed serving dish. Keep hot while you cook the meat.

Fill a deep-frying pan about one-third full with oil and heat it until it reaches 180°C (350°F) on a deep-fat thermometer, or until a small cube of stale bread dropped into the oil turns golden in 55 seconds.

Carefully lower the meat cubes into the oil, a few at a time, and fry for 6 to 8 minutes, or until they are golden brown and crisp. Drain on kitchen towels and, when all the cubes have been cooked, transfer to the centre of the serving dish. Serve at once.

4 Servings

VEAU MARENGO
(Veal Cooked with Mushrooms and Wine)

Legend has it that a version of this recipe (using chicken) was created by Napoleon's cook just after the Battle of Marengo—hence the rather unusual name.

	Metric/U.K.	U.S.
Lean stewing veal, cubed 1½kg/3lb		3lb
Salt and pepper to taste		
Butter	75g/3oz	6 Tbs
Vegetable oil	50ml/2floz	¼ cup
Medium onions, thinly sliced	2	2
Garlic cloves, crushed	2	2
Dry white wine	125ml/4floz	½ cup
Veal or chicken stock	125ml/4floz	½ cup
Bouquet garni	1	1
Canned peeled tomatoes	225g/8oz	8oz
Tomato purée (paste)	65g/2½oz	2½oz
Paprika	1 tsp	1 tsp
Pickling or pearl onions	12	12
Button mushrooms, sliced	350g/12oz	3 cups
Beurre manié (page 64)	1 Tbs	1 Tbs

Rub the veal cubes with salt and pepper.

Melt 50g/2oz (4 tablespoons) of the butter with the oil in a large flameproof casserole. Add the onions and garlic and fry until they are soft. Stir in the veal and fry until the cubes are evenly browned. Pour over the wine and stock and stir in the bouquet garni, tomatoes and can juice, the tomato purée (paste) and paprika. Bring to the boil, reduce the heat to low and simmer the mixture for 1½ hours. Add the onions and simmer for a further 30 minutes or until the meat is cooked through.

Meanwhile, melt the remaining butter in a frying-pan. Add the mushrooms and cook for 3 minutes, stirring frequently. Transfer the mushrooms to a warmed serving dish. When the veal is cooked, transfer the cubes and onions to the serving dish. Keep warm while you finish the sauce.

Remove the casserole from the heat and strain the contents into a saucepan, pressing down on the vegetables and flavourings with the back of a wooden spoon. Skim any scum from the surface of the cooking liquid and bring to the boil. Boil for about 10 minutes, or until the liquid has reduced by about a third. Stir in the beurre manié, a little at a time, and cook the sauce for 2 to 3 minutes, stirring constantly, or until it has thickened and is smooth.

Pour the sauce over the meat and vegetables and serve at once.

6 Servings

ESCALOPES DE VEAU CORDON BLEU

	Metric/U.K.	U.S.
Cooked ham	4 thin slices	4 thin slices
Gruyère cheese	4 thin slices	4 thin slices
Veal escalopes, pounded thin	8	8
Pepper to taste		
Dried marjoram	½ tsp	½ tsp
Flour	25g/1oz	¼ cup
Eggs, lightly beaten	2	2
Dry white breadcrumbs	50g/2oz	⅔ cup
Butter	125g/4oz	8 Tbs
Lemon slices	4	4

Napoleon's cook is reputed to have created a version of this classic on the battlefield of Marengo, hence Veau Marengo. Its a delicious combination of lean veal, white wine, tomatoes, mushrooms and onions.

Put a slice of ham and a slice of cheese on four of the escalopes. Cover with the remaining escalopes to make a 'sandwich'. Pound the edges of the escalopes with a mallet to seal them.

Sprinkle the veal with pepper and the marjoram, then dip them first in the flour, then in the eggs and finally in the breadcrumbs, shaking off any excess. Wrap in greaseproof or waxed paper and chill in the refrigerator for 30 minutes.

Melt the butter in a large frying-pan. Add the escalopes and fry them for 3 minutes on each side. Reduce the heat to low and cook, turning occasionally, for a further 15 minutes, or until the 'sandwiches' are cooked through.

Transfer to a warmed serving dish, garnish with the lemon slices and serve at once.

4 Servings

Cassoulet is one of the great dishes from Languedoc in south western France, Cassoulet de Gascogne is a somewhat simplified but equally tasty version of the classic, from neighbouring Gascony.

ROGNONS DE DIJON
(Kidneys with Mustard Sauce)

	Metric/U.K.	U.S.
Butter	25g/1oz	2 Tbs
Veal kidneys, cleaned and cut into pieces	700g/1½lb	1½lb
Flour	2 Tbs	2 Tbs
Single (light) cream	300ml/10floz	1¼ cups
French mustard	2-3 Tbs	2-3 Tbs
Salt and pepper to taste		
Chopped parsley	6 Tbs	6 Tbs

Melt the butter in a large frying-pan. Add the kidney pieces and fry until they are deeply and evenly browned. Transfer them to a plate.

Remove the pan from the heat and stir in the flour to form a smooth paste. Gradually stir in the cream and mustard and return the pan to the heat. Cook the sauce for 2 to 3 minutes, stirring constantly, or until it is smooth and thick. Stir in the seasoning and parsley. Return the kidneys to the pan and simmer for 5 minutes, or until they are cooked through and tender.

Transfer the mixture to a warmed serving dish and serve at once.

4-6 Servings

FOIE DE VEAU AU VIN BLANC
(Calf's Liver in White Wine)

	Metric/U.K.	U.S.
Calf's liver, thinly sliced	700g/1½lb	1½lb
Seasoned flour (flour with salt and pepper to taste)	50g/2oz	½ cup
Butter	50g/2oz	4 Tbs
Dry white wine	250ml/8floz	1 cup
Single (light) cream	2 Tbs	2 Tbs
Salt and pepper to taste		

Coat the liver slices in the seasoned flour, shaking off any excess.

Melt the butter in a large frying-pan. Add the liver slices and fry for 1 minute on each side. Pour over the wine and bring to the boil. Reduce the heat to low and simmer for 2 minutes, or until the liver is cooked through and tender. Transfer the liver to a warmed serving dish.

Stir the cream and seasoning into the pan and heat gently until hot but not boiling. Pour the sauce over the liver slices and serve at once.

4 Servings

CASSOULET GASCOGNE
(Bean Stew with Sausages and Garlic and Parsley Butter)

	Metric/U.K.	U.S.
Salt pork, cubed	½kg/1lb	1lb
Dried white haricot (dried white) beans, soaked overnight in cold water and drained	½kg/1lb	2⅔ cups
Bouquet garni	1	1
Salt and pepper to taste		
Smoked pork sausages (Italian or Polish), cut into 2½cm/1in pieces	½kg/1lb	1lb
GASCONY BUTTER Salt	½ tsp	½ tsp
Garlic cloves	8	8
Butter	75g/3oz	6 Tbs
French mustard	1 tsp	1 tsp
Chopped parsley	2 Tbs	2 Tbs

Preheat the oven to moderate 180°C (Gas Mark 4, 350°F).

Put the salt pork and beans in a casserole and pour over just enough boiling water to cover. Add the bouquet garni and cover. Put the casserole into the oven and cook for 3 hours, or until the beans are tender. Remove from the oven and add seasoning to taste and the sausage pieces. Return to the oven to cook, uncovered, for a further 30 minutes.

Meanwhile, to make the butter, half-fill a saucepan with water. Add the salt and garlic cloves and bring to the boil. Boil for 10 minutes. Transfer the cloves to a mortar and pound or mash them, with the butter, to form a smooth paste. Stir in the mustard and parsley. Remove the casserole from the oven.

Strain off any liquid and remove the bouquet garni. Stir in the garlic butter and serve.

4 Servings

SAUCISSES A LA PUREE DE CELERI RAVE
(Sausages with Puréed Celeriac)

	Metric/U.K.	U.S.
Water	250ml/8floz	1 cup

	Metric/U.K.	U.S.
Salt and pepper to taste		
Dried marjoram	½ tsp	½ tsp
Grated lemon rind	½ tsp	½ tsp
Potatoes, chopped	½kg/1lb	1lb
Celeriac, sliced	½kg/1lb	1lb
Onion, chopped	1	1
Sausages	4-8	4-8
Hot milk	50ml/2floz	¼ cup
Cheddar or Gruyère cheese, grated	75g/3oz	¾ cup

The French touch with sausages is amply demonstrated in this rustic Saucisses à la Purée de Celeri Rave.

Put the water, seasoning, marjoram and lemon rind into a saucepan and bring to the boil. Add the potatoes, celeriac and onion and reduce the heat to low. Simmer for 20 to 25 minutes, or until the vegetables are cooked through and tender.

Preheat the grill (broiler) to moderate. Arrange the sausages in the lined rack of the grill (broiler) pan and grill (broil) for 6 to 10 minutes, or until they are cooked through.

Drain the vegetables, then purée them in a blender, or rub them through a strainer into a bowl, using the back of a wooden spoon. Stir the hot milk and cheese into the vegetable mixture and beat well until the cheese has melted and the ingredients are thoroughly blended.

Spoon the mixture into a warmed serving dish and top with the sausages. Serve at once.

2-4 Servings

Poultry and Game

liquid into the mixture, then pour the mixture into the saucepan. Simmer gently, stirring constantly, for 3 to 5 minutes, or until the sauce thickens slightly. Take care not to let the sauce boil, or it will curdle.

Pour the sauce over the chicken pieces, sprinkle over the paprika and serve at once.

6 Servings

FRICASSEE DE POULET
(Chicken, Tomato and Mushroom Stew)

In French cooking, a fricassée is simply a white meat stew, cooked in white stock or sauce, and although this version is chicken, lamb and veal are also often cooked in this way.

	Metric/U.K.	U.S.
Chicken, skinned and cut into serving pieces	1x2½kg/5lb	1x5lb
Seasoned flour (flour with salt and pepper to taste)	50g/2oz	½ cup
Vegetable oil	50ml/2floz	¼ cup
Chicken stock	450ml/15floz	2 cups
Cornflour (cornstarch), blended with 1 Tbs water	1½ tsp	1½ tsp
Bay leaf	1	1
Garlic clove, crushed	1	1
Medium tomatoes, blanched, peeled and chopped	6	6
Small button mushrooms, sliced	225g/8oz	2 cups
Egg yolks	2	2
Double (heavy) cream	150ml/5floz	⅝ cup
Paprika	½ tsp	½ tsp

Coat the chicken pieces in the seasoned flour, shaking off any excess.

Heat the oil in a large saucepan. Add the chicken pieces and fry until they are deeply and evenly browned. Stir in the stock, cornflour (cornstarch) mixture, bay leaf and garlic, and bring to the boil.

Reduce the heat to low, cover the pan and simmer for 40 minutes. Stir in the tomatoes and mushrooms and simmer for a further 20 minutes. Remove the bay leaf.

Transfer the chicken pieces to a warmed serving dish.

Combine the egg yolks and cream together. Stir about 4 tablespoons of the chicken cooking

POULET VALLEE D'AUGE
(Chicken with Calvados in Cream)

Normandy is the home of the French dairy industry and also of Calvados, a sort of brandy made from apples, so the two types of ingredients are often incorporated into the food of the region as here.

	Metric/U.K.	U.S.
Butter	50g/2oz	4 Tbs
Roasting chicken	1x1½kg/3lb	1x3lb
Calvados (or brandy if you prefer)	50ml/2floz	¼ cup
Shallots, finely chopped	2	2
Celery stalk, chopped	1	1
Large dessert apple, peeled, cored and chopped	1	1
Streaky (fatty) bacon	50g/2oz	2oz
Dried sage	½ tsp	½ tsp
Salt and pepper to taste		
Dry cider or apple juice	300ml/10floz	1¼ cups
Egg yolks	2	2
Double (heavy) cream	75ml/3floz	⅜ cup

Preheat the oven to warm 170°C (Gas Mark 3, 325°F).

Melt the butter in a large flameproof casserole. Add the chicken and fry until it is evenly browned. Remove from the heat. Warm the Calvados or brandy, pour over the chicken and ignite. When the flames have died down, stir in the vegetables, apple, bacon, sage and seasoning.

Return to the heat and fry the vegetables until they are soft. Pour over the cider or apple juice and bring to the boil. Transfer the casserole to the oven and cook for 1 hour, or until the chicken is cooked through.

Remove the chicken from the casserole and transfer to a warmed serving dish.

Fricassée de Poulet is a classic stew of chicken, tomatoes and mushrooms.

When Rossini became tired of being a musical prodigy he turned to cooking and one of his 'cooking' friends was the great French chef Auguste Escoffier, who created Suprèmes de Volailles Rossini in his honour. It is a stunning mixture of boned chicken breasts with pâté and a Madeira-based sauce.

Strain the cooking liquid into a small saucepan, pressing down on the vegetables and bacon with the back of a wooden spoon to extract all the juice. Boil rapidly until the sauce has reduced by about one-third.

Beat the egg yolks and cream together, then gradually stir in the sauce. Return the sauce to the saucepan and simmer gently until it is hot but not boiling. When the sauce has thickened, pour a little over the chicken and the remainder into a warmed sauceboat. Serve the chicken at once, accompanied by the sauce.

4 Servings

POULET A L'ESTRAGON
(Chicken with Tarragon)

This is one of the classics of French country cuisine. If at all possible, fresh tarragon should be used—the taste will not be nearly so delicate with the dried variety.

	Metric/U.K.	U.S.
Butter, softened	125g/4oz	8 Tbs
Salt and pepper to taste		
Chopped fresh tarragon	4 Tbs	4 Tbs
Roasting chicken	1x2½kg/5lb	1x5lb
Tarragon sprigs	6	6

Preheat the oven to fairly hot 190°C (Gas Mark 5, 375°F).

Combine the butter, seasoning and chopped tarragon and beat until they form a smooth paste. Stuff half the mixture inside the cavity of the chicken and close with trussing thread or a skewer.

Put the chicken into a roasting pan, then spread the remaining butter mixture over the chicken, particularly over the breast area. Put the pan into the oven and roast for 30 minutes, basting occasionally. Turn the chicken over on to the other side and return to the oven to roast for a further 30 minutes, basting occasionally.

Reduce the oven temperature to moderate

180°C (Gas Mark 4, 350°F). Turn the chicken on to its back and baste well with the melted butter. Roast for a further 30 minutes, basting well, or until the chicken is cooked through and tender.

Remove from the oven and transfer the chicken to a warmed serving dish. Pour the cooking juices over the chicken, garnish with the tarragon sprigs and serve at once.

6 Servings

POULET BONNE FEMME
(Chicken Casserole with Vegetables)

Bonne femme in French means 'good wife' and obviously (in France at least!) the function of a 'good' wife is very much wrapped up with the art of producing good cooking, economically and with little apparent effort. This dish fully merits the description, being economical, unbelievably good to eat—and a nourishingly balanced meal.

	Metric/U.K.	U.S.
Chicken	1x2kg/4lb	1x4lb
Salt and pepper to taste		
Butter	50g/2oz	4 Tbs
Pickling or pearl onions	700g/1½lb	1½lb
Small new potatoes, scrubbed	700g/1½lb	1½lb
Lean bacon, chopped	6 slices	6 slices
Bouquet garni	1	1

Preheat the oven to moderate 180°C (Gas Mark 4, 350°F).

Rub the chicken, inside and out, with salt and pepper.

Melt the butter in a large flameproof casserole. Add the chicken and fry until it is evenly browned. Remove from the casserole. Add the onions, potatoes and bacon and fry for 10 minutes, shaking the casserole frequently so that the bacon does not stick to the bottom.

Return the chicken to the casserole and add seasoning to taste and the bouquet garni. Cover and put into the oven. Cook for 1 hour, or until the chicken is cooked through and tender.

Remove from the oven and remove the bouquet garni. Transfer the chicken to a warmed serving dish and surround with the vegetables and bacon. Serve at once.

4 Servings

SUPREMES DE VOLAILLE ROSSINI
(Boned Chicken Breasts with Pâté)

Auguste Escoffier, by common consent, is one of the two or three most important figures in French cuisine. He lived on into the first years of the 20th century but most of his great masterpieces were created during the Belle Epoque of late 19th century Paris. His abiding interest in music is illustrated in this delicate recipe, dedicated to the Italian composer and chef, Rossini.

	Metric/U.K.	U.S.
Chicken breasts, skinned and boned	6	6
Salt and pepper to taste		
Lemon juice	1 Tbs	1 Tbs
Butter	75g/3oz	6 Tbs
Pâté de foie gras, cut into 6 slices	225g/8oz	8oz
SAUCE		
Medium onion, thinly sliced	1	1
Medium carrot, thinly sliced	1	1
Lean cooked ham, finely chopped	50g/2oz	2oz
Chopped parsley	2 Tbs	2 Tbs
Beef stock	300ml/10floz	1¼ cups
Madeira	50ml/2floz	¼ cup
Beurre manié (page 64)	1 Tbs	1 Tbs

Rub the breasts with salt, pepper and lemon juice.

Melt the butter in a large, deep frying-pan. Add the breasts and fry for 7 to 10 minutes on each side, or until they are cooked through and tender. Transfer the breasts to a warmed serving dish and keep hot while you make the sauce.

Pour off all but 2 tablespoons of the butter. Add the onion, carrot, ham and parsley and fry until the onion is soft. Pour in the stock and Madeira, and bring to the boil, stirring frequently. Strain the liquid into a saucepan, rubbing the vegetables and ham through with the back of a wooden spoon. Return the pan to the heat and bring to the boil. Reduce the heat to low and stir in the beurre manié, a little at a time, until the sauce thickens and is smooth.

Top each chicken breast with a slice of pâté

and pour half the sauce over the top. Pour the remaining sauce into a warmed sauceboat and serve with the meat.

6 Servings

CANETON AUX NAVETS
(Braised Duckling with Turnips)

	Metric/U.K.	U.S.
Duckling, oven-ready and with the giblets reserved	1x2½kg/5lb	1x5lb
Salt and pepper to taste		
Butter	75g/3oz	6 Tbs
Dry white wine	250ml/8floz	1 cup
Duck stock, made with the reserved giblets	350ml/12floz	1½ cups
Bouquets garnis	2	2
Pickling or pearl onions	16	16
Soft brown sugar	2 tsp	2 tsp
Small white turnips, quartered	1kg/2lb	2lb
Lemon juice	½ tsp	½ tsp
Cornflour (cornstarch), blended with 2 Tbs water	2 Tbs	2 Tbs
Chopped parsley	1 Tbs	1 Tbs

Preheat the oven to hot 220°C (Gas Mark 7, 425°F).

Rub the duck all over with salt and pepper.

Melt a third of the butter in a large flame-proof casserole. Add the duck and fry until it is evenly browned. Pour over the wine and stock, and add the bouquets garnis and seasoning. Bring to the boil, then transfer the casserole to the oven. Braise the duck for 30 minutes.

Meanwhile, melt another third of the butter in a frying-pan. Add the onions and half the sugar and fry gently for 5 minutes. Transfer the onions to a plate. Melt the remaining butter in the pan and add the turnips and remaining sugar. Fry gently until the turnips are evenly

A succulent, economical country dish—Caneton aux Navets.

browned. Transfer the turnips to the onions.

Reduce the oven temperature to warm 170°C (Gas Mark 3, 325°F). Arrange the vegetables around the duck, cover and return the casserole to the oven. Braise for a further 1 to 1¼ hours, or until the duck is cooked through and tender. Transfer the duck to a warmed serving dish and untruss. Transfer the onions and turnips to the dish and arrange them decoratively around the duck. Keep hot while you make the sauce.

Strain the cooking liquid into a saucepan and bring to the boil. Boil rapidly for 5 minutes, or until it has reduced by about a third. Stir in the lemon juice and seasoning. Stir in the cornflour (cornstarch) until the sauce has thickened and is smooth.

Pour the sauce into a warmed sauceboat and serve at once, with the duck and vegetables. Garnish with the parsley.

4 Servings

PINTADES FARCIES
(Stuffed Guinea Fowls)

	Metric/U.K.	U.S.
Minced (ground) veal	225g/8oz	8oz
Chicken livers, coarsely chopped	175g/6oz	6oz
Shelled pistachio nuts	25g/1oz	¼ cup
Fresh parsley	1 Tbs	1 Tbs
Chopped fresh tarragon	1 Tbs	1 Tbs
Salt and pepper to taste		
Brandy	1 Tbs	1 Tbs
Guinea fowls, cleaned and boned	2x700g/1½lb	2x1½lb
Streaky (fatty) bacon	6 slices	6 slices
Butter	125g/4oz	8 Tbs
Medium onion, thinly sliced	1	1

Another example of the elegance and superlative taste of haute cuisine at its best, Pintades Farcies (stuffed guinea fowls).

	Metric/U.K.	U.S.
Dried thyme	½ tsp	½ tsp
Bay leaf	1	1
Chicken stock	250ml/8floz	1 cup
Mushrooms, with stalks removed	½kg/1lb	4 cups
Egg yolk	1	1
Double (heavy) cream	2 Tbs	2 Tbs

Combine the veal, chicken livers, nuts, herbs, seasoning and brandy together.

Lay the guinea fowls out flat on a working surface and spoon half the stuffing mixture into each one. Wrap the guinea fowls around the stuffing and sew them up with a trussing needle and thread. Place three bacon slices over the breast of each fowl and tie them on with string.

Melt half the butter in a large flameproof casserole. Add the guinea fowls and fry until they are evenly browned. Add the onion, herbs and stock and bring to the boil. Reduce the heat to low, cover and simmer for 50 minutes to 1 hour, or until the fowls are cooked through and tender.

Five minutes before the end of the cooking time, melt the remaining butter in a saucepan. Add the mushrooms and cook for 3 minutes. Remove the pan from the heat.

Remove the casserole from the heat and carefully transfer the guinea fowls to a warmed serving dish. Remove the bacon slices. Arrange the mushrooms around the fowls and keep hot while you make the sauce.

Strain the cooking liquid into a saucepan skimming any scum from the surface. Bring to the boil.

Combine the egg yolk and cream in a small bowl. Stir in about 4 tablespoons of the stock, then pour the mixture into the saucepan. Simmer gently for 3 minutes, or until the sauce has thickened and is smooth. Do not let the sauce boil or it will curdle.

Pour the sauce into a warmed sauceboat and serve at once, with the stuffed guinea fowls.

6 Servings

SALMIS DE PIGEONS
(Pigeon Stew)

	Metric/U.K.	U.S.
Pigeons, oven-ready with the giblets reserved	6	6
Salt and pepper to taste		
Butter, melted	175g/6oz	12 Tbs
Streaky (fatty) bacon	6 slices	6 slices
Button mushrooms, cooked and drained	125g/4oz	1 cup
Brandy	50ml/2floz	¼ cup
Truffle, drained and thinly sliced	1	1
SAUCE		
Onion, finely chopped	1	1
Medium carrot, chopped	1	1
Bouquet garni	1	1
Chicken stock	250ml/8floz	1 cup
Dry white wine	250ml/8floz	1 cup
Butter	25g/1oz	2 Tbs
Flour	25g/1oz	¼ cup
Salt and pepper to taste		

Preheat the oven to moderate 180°C (Gas Mark 4, 350°F).

Rub the pigeons, inside and out, with salt and pepper. Place them in a large roasting pan and spoon over the melted butter. Lay a slice of bacon over the breast of each bird. Put the pan into the oven and roast for 40 minutes.

Remove the pan from the oven and remove the bacon from the birds. Transfer the pigeons to a carving board. Skin the pigeons and carve the meat into slices. Arrange the slices in a large flameproof casserole. Cover with mushrooms and sprinkle with half the brandy. Place the truffle slices on top of the mushrooms and sprinkle with the remaining brandy. Set aside while you prepare the sauce.

Chop the pigeon skin and giblets finely.

Pour off all but 125ml/4floz (½ cup) of the cooking liquid from the pan. Strain these juices into a saucepan. Set over moderate heat and add the skin, giblets, the carcasses, onion, carrot and bouquet garni. Pour in the stock and wine, and bring to the boil. Cover and simmer the mixture for 15 minutes, or until it has reduced by about a quarter. Remove from the heat and strain the liquid into a large bowl, pressing down on the ingredients with the back of a wooden spoon to extract all the juices. Skim off any scum from the surface of the strained liquid.

Melt the butter in a small saucepan. Remove from the heat and stir in the flour to form a smooth paste. Gradually stir in the strained liquid and return to the heat. Bring to the boil,

stirring constantly. Cook for 2 to 3 minutes, stirring constantly, or until the sauce is thick and smooth. Season to taste.

Pour the sauce over the pigeon meat, cover and set over moderately low heat. Simmer for 15 minutes. Remove from the heat and transfer the meat to a warmed serving dish. Arrange the mushrooms and truffle around it and pour over half the sauce. Pour the remaining sauce into a warmed sauceboat and serve at once, with the meat and vegetables.

4-6 Servings

LAPIN A LA SAUCE MOUTARDE
(Rabbit with Mustard Sauce)

	Metric/U.K.	U.S.
Rabbit, cleaned and cut into serving pieces	1x2kg/4lb	1x4lb
Butter	50g/2oz	4 Tbs
Salt and pepper to taste		
Dried thyme	½ tsp	½ tsp
Dried rosemary	½ tsp	½ tsp
Single (light) cream	300ml/10floz	1¼ cups
French mustard	1 Tbs	1 Tbs
Cornflour (cornstarch), blended with 2 Tbs single (light) cream	1 Tbs	1 Tbs
MARINADE		
Dry white wine	300ml/10floz	1¼ cups
Olive oil	125ml/4floz	½ cup
Garlic cloves, crushed	2	2
Salt and pepper to taste		
Medium onion, thinly sliced	1	1
Medium carrot, thinly sliced	1	1

To prepare the marinade, mix all the ingredients in a large, shallow bowl. Add the rabbit pieces and marinate them at room temperature for 6 hours, basting occasionally. Remove the rabbit from the marinade and dry on kitchen towels. Reserve the marinade.

Melt the butter in a large, deep frying-pan. Add the rabbit pieces and fry until they are evenly browned. Pour in the marinade and bring to the boil. Stir in seasoning, cover and simmer for 1 to 1¼ hours, or until the pieces are cooked through and tender. Remove the pan from the heat and transfer the rabbit to a warmed serving dish. Keep warm while you make the sauce.

Strain the cooking liquids into a small saucepan, pressing down on the vegetables with the back of a wooden spoon. Bring to the boil, then stir in the herbs. Reduce the heat to low and stir in the cream, a little at a time, then the mustard and cornflour (cornstarch) mixture. Gently warm the sauce, stirring constantly, until it is hot but not boiling, and is thick.

Pour the sauce into a warmed sauceboat and serve at once, with the rabbit.

4 Servings

Rabbit is an under-used meat in most parts of the English-speaking world, but in France its succulence is much appreciated. In Lapin à la Sauce Moutarde it is teamed with a creamy mustard sauce.

Vegetables and Salads

PAIN DE CHOU FLEUR
(Cauliflower Loaf)

	Metric/U.K.	U.S.
Medium cauliflowers, separated into flowerets	2	2
Potatoes, cooked and quartered	700g/1½lb	1½ lb
Butter	15g/½oz	1 Tbs
Salt and pepper to taste		
Cayenne pepper	¼ tsp	¼ tsp
Eggs	6	6
Gruyère cheese, finely grated	150g/5oz	1¼ cups

Put the cauliflowers into a large saucepan and add just enough water to cover. Bring to the boil and cook for 12 to 15 minutes, or until the flowerets are very tender. Drain and set aside.

Preheat the oven to moderate 180°C (Gas Mark 4, 350°F).

Put the cauliflowers, potatoes, butter, seasoning and cayenne into a bowl and mash together to form a purée. Add the eggs, one by one, beating well between each addition. Alternatively, purée the cauliflowers with the potatoes, butter, seasonings and eggs in a blender.

Stir in 125g/4oz (1 cup) of the grated cheese and spoon the purée into a well-greased medium ovenproof mould. Cover with foil and put the mould into a roasting pan one-third full of boiling water. Put the pan into the oven and bake for 1 hour.

Remove the pan from the oven and remove the mould from the pan. Remove the foil. Place a heatproof serving dish over the top of the mould and invert quickly. The mould should slide out easily. Sprinkle the remaining cheese over the top and return the mould to the oven for 5 minutes, or until the cheese melts.

Remove from the oven and serve at once.

4-6 Servings

Line a large flameproof casserole with the bacon slices. Add the cabbage, then the onions, garlic and seasoning. Moisten with the wine and stock and bring to the boil. Stir in the chestnuts, cover and put into the oven. Braise for 2 to 2½ hours, or until the cabbage is cooked through and most of the liquid is absorbed.

Remove from the oven and serve at once.

6 Servings

PETITS POIS A LA FRANCAISE
(Small Garden Peas, French Style)

	Metric/U.K.	U.S.
Fresh garden peas, weighed after shelling, or frozen petits pois	700g/1½lb	1½lb
Salt and pepper to taste		
Sugar	1 tsp	1 tsp
Medium onion, thinly sliced	1	1
Lettuce leaves, shredded	4	4
Beurre manié (page 64)	25g/1oz	2 Tbs

Put the peas, seasoning, sugar, onion and lettuce into a saucepan. Pour over enough hot water just to cover the peas and bring to the boil. Reduce the heat to very low, cover and simmer the mixture for 20 to 30 minutes, or until the onion is soft and the peas are very tender. Stir in the beurre manié, a little at a time, until the mixture has thickened and is smooth. Simmer for 1 minute.

Remove from the heat and transfer to a warmed serving bowl. Serve at once.

4 Servings

far left: *Pain de Chou Fleur, a delicate vegetable dish with a cauliflower base.*

near left: *Petits Pois à la Française, one of the most famous of French vegetable dishes, a marvellous combination of fresh peas, onion and lettuce.*

CHOU ROUGE A LA LIMOUSINE
(Red Cabbage with Chestnuts)

The delicious combination of red cabbage and chestnuts is a common one in France—this version is a southwestern one, from the province of Limousin. If you prefer, use canned whole chestnuts instead of as suggested here—and in this case, they should be added to the casserole about 30 minutes before the end.

	Metric/U.K.	U.S.
Streaky (fatty) bacon	6 slices	6 slices
Red cabbage, shredded	1kg/2lb	2lb
Medium onions, finely chopped	2	2
Garlic cloves, crushed	2	2
Salt and pepper to taste		
Red wine	150ml/5floz	⅝ cup
Beef stock	150ml/5floz	⅝ cup
chestnuts, blanched and peeled	20	20

Preheat the oven to warm 170°C (Gas Mark 3, 325°F).

CAROTTES VICHY
(Glazed Carrots)

	Metric/U.K.	U.S.
Carrots, thinly sliced	1kg/2lb	2lb
Water	250ml/8floz	1 cup
Butter	50g/2oz	4 Tbs
Sugar	2 Tbs	2 Tbs
Salt	½ tsp	½ tsp

	Metric/U.K.	U.S.
Chopped parsley	2 Tbs	2 Tbs

Put all the ingredients, except the parsley, into a saucepan and bring to the boil. Simmer, uncovered, for 15 minutes, or until the carrots are tender and the liquid has evaporated, shaking the pan frequently so that the carrots are thoroughly glazed.

Transfer to a warmed serving dish and sprinkle over the parsley. Serve at once.

4-6 Servings

RATATOUILLE
(Mixed Vegetable Casserole)

This colourful mixture of peppers, aubergine (eggplant), courgettes (zucchini) and tomatoes is one of the glories of Provençal cooking. It can be served hot or cold. A 425g/14oz can of tomatoes, with its juice, may be substituted for the fresh tomatoes.

	Metric/U.K.	U.S.
Olive oil	125ml/4floz	½ cup
Medium onions, thinly sliced	3	3
Garlic cloves, crushed	2	2
Medium aubergines (eggplants), sliced and dégorged	2	2
Large green pepper, pith and seeds removed and chopped	1	1
Large red pepper, pith and seeds removed and chopped	1	1
Medium courgettes (zucchini), sliced	4	4
Tomatoes, blanched, peeled, seeded and chopped	6	6
Dried basil	1 tsp	1 tsp
Dried rosemary	1 tsp	1 tsp
Salt and pepper to taste		

Heat the oil in a flameproof casserole. Add the onions and garlic and fry until they are soft. Stir in the aubergines (eggplants), peppers and courgettes (zucchini) and fry for 5 minutes. Stir in the remaining ingredients and bring to

the boil. Cover and simmer for 45 minutes to 1 hour, or until the vegetables are tender but still firm.

Serve at once, if you are serving hot.

4-6 Servings

COURGETTES SAUTEES MAITRE D'HOTEL
(Courgettes [Zucchini] with Lemon, Butter and Parsley Sauce)

Maître d'Hotel is served in many ways in France —as a butter on steaks and chops, as a sauce on fish and vegetables. This combination is a particularly successful one.

	Metric/U.K.	U.S.
Butter	75g/3oz	6 Tbs
Courgettes (zucchini), thinly sliced	8	8
Olive oil	2 Tbs	2 Tbs
Lemon juice	2 Tbs	2 Tbs
Salt and pepper to taste		
Chopped parsley	3 Tbs	3 Tbs

Melt two-thirds of the butter in a large frying-pan. Add the courgette (zucchini) slices to the pan and cook for 8 to 10 minutes, turning occasionally, or until they are evenly browned and cooked through.

Stir in the lemon juice and seasoning, then the remaining butter and parsley. When the butter has melted, transfer the mixture to a warmed serving dish.

Serve at once.

4 Servings

POMMES DE TERRE SOUFFLEES
(Potato Puffs)

	Metric/U.K.	U.S.
Potatoes, cut into ¼cm/⅛in slices	½kg/1lb	1lb
Sufficient vegetable oil for deep-frying		
Salt	1 tsp	1 tsp

Put the slices into a large bowl of water and set aside for 30 minutes. Drain and dry thoroughly on kitchen towels.

Fill two large saucepans one-third full with oil. Heat the oil in one pan until it reaches 170°C (325°F) on a deep-fat thermometer, or until a small cube of stale bread dropped into the oil turns golden in 65 seconds. Heat the oil in the second pan until it reaches 190°C (375°F) on a deep-fat thermometer or until a small cube of stale bread dropped into the oil turns golden in 40 seconds.

Drop the potato slices into the first pan and fry for 4 minutes. Using a slotted spoon, transfer the slices to the second pan and fry for 2 to 3 minutes or until they puff up. Remove from the oil and drain on kitchen towels.

Sprinkle over the salt and serve at once.

2-4 Servings

POMMES DE TERRE AU ROQUEFORT
(Baked Potatoes with Blue Cheese)

Roquefort is rather an expensive cheese outside France, certainly to use in cooking, so for economy's sake, any type of blue cheese may be substituted if you prefer.

	Metric/U.K.	U.S.
Large potatoes, scrubbed	4	4
Sour cream	150ml/5floz	$\frac{5}{8}$ cup
Roquefort cheese, crumbled	125g/4oz	4oz
Chopped chives	2 Tbs	2 Tbs
Pinch of cayenne pepper		
Salt and pepper to taste		

Preheat the oven to fairly hot 190°C (Gas Mark 5, 375°F).

Put the potatoes on a baking sheet and put them into the oven. Bake for 1 to 1½ hours, or until they are cooked through. (Cooking times will depend on the size of the potatoes.)

Remove the potatoes from the oven and set aside to cool a little. When they are cool enough to handle, lay them on their sides. Cut off a thin slice, lengthways, from the top of each potato and, using a spoon, carefully scoop out the inside to within ½cm/¼in of the shell, leaving the shell intact.

Two delicious recipes with potato : Pommes de Terre au Roquefort (baked potato with a blue cheese stuffing) and Pommes de Terre Soufflés (deep-fried potato puffs).

49

Mash together the scooped out potato flesh, sour cream, cheese, chives, cayenne and seasoning. Stuff equal amounts into the potato shells and return the stuffed potatoes to the baking sheet. Bake for 10 to 15 minutes, or until the top of the filling is lightly browned.

Remove from the oven and serve at once.

4 Servings

SALADE DE RIZ AU SAUCISSON
(Rice Salad with Garlic Sausage)

	Metric/U.K.	U.S.
Long-grain rice, soaked in cold water for 30 minutes and drained	125g/4oz	⅔ cup
Salt and black pepper to taste		
Mayonnaise	75ml/3floz	⅜ cup
Dried chervil	1 tsp	1 tsp
½ red pepper, pith and seeds removed and and chopped	½	½
Hard-boiled eggs	2	2
Small lettuce, separated into leaves	1	1
Garlic sausage, cut into ½cm/¼in slices	1x20cm/8in	1x8in

Put the rice into a saucepan. Pour over enough water to cover and add about a teaspoon of salt. Bring to the boil, cover and reduce the heat to low. Simmer for 15 to 20 minutes, or until the rice is cooked and all the liquid is absorbed. Transfer the rice to a large bowl and set aside for 5 minutes.

Meanwhile, mix together the seasoning, mayonnaise and chervil. Pour half over the rice and add the red pepper. Using two large spoons, carefullly toss the mixture to blend. Set aside to cool completely.

Meanwhile, cut the eggs in half, lengthways. Remove the yolks and add them to the remaining mayonnaise mixture. Mash well, then return the mixture to the egg whites. Arrange the lettuce leaves in a salad bowl. Pile the rice mixture on top and arrange the sausage slices around the edges. Garnish with the filled egg whites and serve the salad at once.

4-6 Servings

CAROTTES RAPEES
(Grated Carrot Salad)

	Metric/U.K.	U.S.
Carrots	½kg/1lb	1lb
DRESSING		
Olive oil	3 Tbs	3 Tbs
White wine vinegar	1½ Tbs	1½ Tbs
Lemon juice	1 tsp	1 tsp
Sugar	½ tsp	½ tsp
Salt and pepper to taste		

First make the dressing. Put all the ingredients into a screw-topped jar and shake vigorously.

Grate the carrots into a shallow salad bowl. Pour over the dressing and, using two large spoons, carefully toss to blend thoroughly.

Cover and chill before serving.

4 Servings

SALADE NICOISE
(Potato, French Bean and Tomato Salad)

	Metric/U.K.	U.S.
Small lettuce, separated into leaves	1	1
Medium cold cooked potatoes, diced	6	6
Cold cooked French beans, cut into lengths	275g/10oz	1⅔ cups
Tomatoes, blanched, peeled and quartered	6	6
Garlic cloves, crushed	2	2
Anchovy fillets, halved	6	6
Black olives, stoned	10	10
Capers	2 Tbs	2 Tbs
DRESSING		
Olive oil	50ml/2floz	¼ cup
Wine vinegar	2 Tbs	2 Tbs
French mustard	1 tsp	1 tsp

Arrange the lettuce leaves in a large salad bowl.

Put the potatoes, beans, tomatoes and garlic into the centre of the bowl. Combine all the ingredients for the dressing together, then pour over the vegetables. Garnish with the anchovies, olives and capers.

6 Servings

An unusual and colourful salad meal in itself, Salade de Riz au Saucisson.

Eggs and Cheese

SOUFFLE DE FROMAGE
(Cheese Soufflé)

	Metric/U.K.	U.S.
Butter	50g/2oz	4 Tbs
Cheese, grated (preferably a mixture of Gruyère and Parmesan)	150g/5oz	1¼ cups
Flour	25g/1oz	4 Tbs
Milk, scalded	300ml/10floz	1¼ cups
Salt and pepper to taste		
Paprika	¼ tsp	¼ tsp
Egg yolks	5	5
Egg whites	6	6
Cream of tartar	¼ tsp	¼ tsp

Preheat the oven to moderate 180°C (Gas Mark 4, 350°F). Using a little of the butter, grease a medium soufflé dish. Sprinkle about 4 tablespoons of the grated cheese around the inside and press on to the bottom and sides.

Melt the remaining butter in a saucepan. Remove the pan from the heat and stir in the flour to form a smooth paste. Gradually stir in the scalded milk and return to the heat. Bring to the boil and cook the sauce, stirring constantly, for 2 to 3 minutes, or until it is thick and smooth.

Remove from the heat again and beat in the seasoning and paprika, then the egg yolks a little at a time. Set aside to cool slightly.

Beat the egg whites until they are foamy. Add salt to taste and the cream of tartar and continue to beat until they form stiff peaks.

Stir the remaining cheese into the egg yolk mixture and when it is thoroughly blended, quickly fold in the egg whites. Transfer the mixture to the prepared soufflé dish. Carefully mark a deep circle in the centre of the soufflé and place the dish in the oven. Bake for 40 to 45 minutes, or until it is lightly browned on top and the soufflé is well risen.

Remove from the oven and serve at once.

4-6 Servings

OMELETTE FINES HERBES
(Omelet with Fresh Herbs)

Fines Herbes is one of the classic fillings for omelets in France and the herbs involved are usually a combination of parsley, chervil and tarragon. Chives and occasionally bay leaves are also sometimes added. If you are going to make this recipe, it is essential that fresh herbs be used to attain the full, delicate taste.

	Metric/U.K.	U.S.
Eggs	6	6
Salt and pepper to taste		
Cold water	2 Tbs	2 Tbs
Chopped fresh herbs	1½ Tbs	1½ Tbs
Butter	15g/½oz	1 Tbs

Beat the eggs, seasoning, water and herbs together until they are thoroughly blended.

Melt the butter in a large omelet pan. Pour in the egg mixture. Stir, then leave for a few seconds until the bottom sets. Reduce the heat to low. Using a palette knife or spatula, lift the edges of the omelet and, at the same time, tilt the pan away from you so that the liquid egg escapes from the top and runs on to the pan. Put the pan down flat over the heat and leave until the omelet begins to set again. Tilt the pan away from you again and, with the help of the knife, flip one half of the omelet over to make a semi-circle.

Remove from the heat and slide the omelet on to a warmed serving dish. Serve at once.

3 Servings

OEUFS ST. GERMAIN
(Eggs with Purée of Peas)

	Metric/U.K.	U.S.
Fresh peas, weighed after shelling	½kg/1lb	1lb
Butter	65g/2½oz	5 Tbs
Chicken stock	65ml/2½floz	⅓ cup
Onion, very finely chopped	1	1
Large lettuce leaves, shredded	4	4
Salt and pepper to taste		
Medium potatoes	2	2

Eggs, soft-boiled	6	6
Triangles of fried bread (to garnish)		

Put the peas in a saucepan and just cover with cold water. Bring to the boil, then remove from the heat and drain. Return the peas to the pan and add the butter, stock, onion, lettuce and seasoning. Cover and simmer until the peas are tender and most of the liquid has been absorbed.

Meanwhile, boil the potatoes in salted water for 15 to 20 minutes, or until they are tender. Drain and either purée in a blender or push through a strainer. Transfer to a bowl. Purée the peas in a blender or push them through the strainer. Stir the pea mixture into the potatoes, then season to taste.

Divide the purée among individual serving plates and arrange a shelled egg on top.

Garnish with the bread triangles and serve at once.

6 Servings

QUICHE LORRAINE
(Bacon and Egg Flan)

This is virtually the national dish of Lorraine, on the border with Germany. Almost as many versions exist as there are villages in the region, but this is a fairly typical version.

	Metric/U.K.	U.S.
Shortcrust pastry dough	275g/10oz	10oz
FILLING		
Smoked or unsmoked bacon, grilled (broiled)		

Quiches are part and parcel of French life and they can have many different fillings. This particular filling is courgettes (zucchini) and tomatoes.

until crisp and crumbled	175g/6oz	6oz
Single (light) cream	250ml/8floz	1 cup
Egg yolks	3	3
Salt and pepper to taste		

Preheat the oven to fairly hot 200°C (Gas Mark 6, 400°F).

Roll out the pastry dough to about $\frac{1}{2}$cm/$\frac{1}{4}$in thick and use it to line a well-greased 23cm/9in flan tin. Put the tin on a baking sheet. Arrange the crumbled bacon over the bottom of the case.

Beat the remaining ingredients together and pour over the bacon. Put the baking sheet into the oven and bake the quiche for 25 to 30 minutes, or until the filling is set and firm and golden brown on top.

Serve at once, if you are serving the quiche hot, or set aside to cool before serving.

4-6 Servings

QUICHE AUX COURGETTES ET TOMATES
(Courgette [Zucchini] and Tomato Flan)

	Metric/U.K.	U.S.
Shortcrust pastry dough	275g/10oz	10oz
FILLING		
Butter	50g/2oz	4 Tbs
Garlic cloves, crushed	2	2
Courgettes (zucchini), sliced	4	4
Salt and pepper to taste		
Single (light) cream	125ml/4floz	$\frac{1}{2}$ cup
Eggs	3	3
Gruyère or Cheddar cheese, grated	50g/2oz	$\frac{1}{2}$ cup
Small tomatoes, blanched, peeled and thinly sliced	5	5

Preheat the oven to fairly hot 200°C (Gas Mark 6, 400°F).

Roll out the pastry dough to about $\frac{1}{2}$cm/$\frac{1}{4}$in thick and use it to line a well-greased 23cm/9in flan tin. Put the tin on a baking sheet.

Melt the butter in a large frying-pan. Add the garlic and fry for 1 minute. Add the courgette (zucchini) slices and seasoning to taste. Cook for 8 to 10 minutes, or until they are evenly browned. Remove from the heat.

Beat the cream, eggs and grated cheese together.

Arrange the courgettes (zucchini) and tomatoes in concentric circles in the flan case. Pour over the cream mixture. Put the baking sheet into the oven and bake the quiche for 35 to 40 minutes, or until the filling is set and firm and golden brown on top.

Remove from the oven and serve at once, if you are serving the quiche hot, or set aside to cool before serving.

4-6 Servings

CREPES AU FROMAGE
(Blue Cheese Crêpes)

Crêpes are very popular all over France although they originate in Brittany. This one is a delicious combination of crêpes and the queen of French blue cheeses, Roquefort.

	Metric/U.K.	U.S.
Béchamel sauce (page 64)	250ml/8floz	1 cup
Egg yolk	1	1
Roquefort cheese, crumbled	150g/5oz	5oz
Salt and pepper to taste		
Crêpe batter (savoury) (page 64)	225g/8oz	1 cup
Butter, melted	25g/1oz	2 Tbs
Brandy, warmed	50ml/2floz	$\frac{1}{4}$ cup

To make the filling, pour the béchamel and egg yolk into a bowl and beat together until they are thoroughly blended. Stir in the crumbled cheese and seasoning and beat well to blend. Chill in the refrigerator for 1 hour.

Fry the crêpes according to the instructions in the batter recipe.

Lay the crêpes out flat and put about 2 tablespoons of the filling in the centre of each one. Fold in half, then in quarters to enclose the filling.

Arrange the crêpes on a chafing dish or baking dish and pour over the melted butter. Pour over the warmed brandy and ignite. Shake gently until the flames have died away, then serve at once.

6 Servings

Desserts and Cakes

BAVAROIS AU CHOCOLAT
(Chocolate Bavarian Cream)

This richly flavoured dessert belongs firmly in the tradition of grand cuisine; its origins are very old, but the dessert was revived and refined by the great Careme and is now the glory of many an haute cuisine restaurant.

	Metric/U.K.	U.S.
Vegetable oil	1 Tbs	1 Tbs
Milk	725ml/1¼ pints	3 cups
Dark cooking (semi-sweet) chocolate, grated	125g/4oz	4 squares
Castor (superfine) sugar	75g/3oz	⅜ cup
Egg yolks	4	4
Gelatine	15g/½oz	½oz
Strong black coffee	125ml/4floz	½ cup
Vanilla essence (extract)	1 tsp	1 tsp
Double (heavy) cream, beaten until thick	150ml/5floz	⅝ cup
Rum	2 Tbs	2 Tbs

One of the glories of French cuisine, now appreciated the whole world over—Crème Caramel.

Grease the inside of a 1¼l/2 pint (1½ quart) mould with the oil, then place upside down on kitchen towels to drain off any excess. Set aside.

Put the milk and chocolate into a saucepan and cook over low heat, stirring constantly until the chocolate has dissolved. Remove from the heat.

Put the sugar into a heatproof bowl. Make a well in the centre and drop in the egg yolks, one at a time, beating slowly until the sugar has been completely incorporated. Pour over the milk mixture in a thin steady stream, beating constantly. Put the bowl over a saucepan half-filled with hot water and set the pan over low heat. Cook, stirring constantly, until the custard is thick enough to coat the back of a wooden spoon. Do not let the mixture boil or it will curdle. Remove from the heat.

Dissolve the gelatine in the coffee over low heat, then stir into the custard. Strain the custard into a bowl placed over crushed ice. Stir constantly until the custard thickens.

Beat the vanilla into the cream then, using a metal spoon, lightly fold the cream mixture and rum into the thickening custard. Pour the mixture into the prepared mould.

Cover the mould with foil or greaseproof or waxed paper and transfer to the refrigerator to chill for 6 hours, or until the mould has completely set.

Remove from the refrigerator and run a knife around the edge of the cream. Quickly dip the bottom of the mould in hot water and invert quickly on to a serving dish, giving the bottom a sharp tap. The cream should slide out easily.

Serve at once.

4-6 Servings

CREME CARAMEL
(Baked Caramel Custard)

	Metric/U.K.	U.S.
Sugar	125g/4oz	½ cup
Water	65ml/2½floz	⅓ cup
CREME		
Milk	600ml/1 pint	2½ cups
Sugar	90g/3½oz	Scant ½ cup
Eggs	2	2
Egg yolks	2	2
Vanilla essence (extract)	1 tsp	1 tsp

Dissolve the sugar in the water over low heat, stirring constantly until it has dissolved. Increase the heat to moderately high and bring to the boil. Cook for 3 to 4 minutes, without stirring, or until it turns a light nut-brown colour. (Be careful not to overcook or the syrup will darken too much and become bitter.) Pour into individual ramekin dishes or a heatproof dish. Dissolve the milk and sugar together, stirring constantly. Remove from the heat.

Beat the eggs and egg yolks together in a bowl until they thicken and become pale yellow. Stir in the milk and vanilla.

Preheat the oven to warm 170°C (Gas Mar, 3, 325°F).

Strain the mixture into the ramekins or dish, spooning off any froth which appears on the surface. Put the dishes or dish into a roasting pan and add enough boiling water to come halfway up the sides.

Put the pan into the oven and bake the crème for 40 minutes, or until the centres are firm when pressed with your fingertip. Do not allow the water to boil during baking or the custard will have a grainy texture. (If it does begin to boil, reduce the temperature.)

Bavarois au Chocolat, the perfect end to any meal.

Remove the dishes or dish from the water and set aside to cool completely. Chill in the refrigerator for 1 hour.

Run a knife around the edge of the ramekins or dish and invert on to serving plates. Serve at once.

6 Servings

To serve, remove the mould from the refrigerator and run a knife around the edge of the rice. Invert quickly on to a serving dish, giving the mould a sharp tap. The rice should slide out easily.

Serve at once.

6 Servings

RIZ A L'IMPERATRICE
(Empress Rice Pudding)

This delicious dessert is said to have been created for, and named after, the Empress Eugenie, wife of Napoleon III of France.

	Metric/U.K.	U.S.
Round-grain rice	75g/3oz	½ cup
Castor (superfine) sugar	50g/2oz	¼ cup
Milk	900ml/1½ pints	3¾ cups
Vanilla essence (extract)	1½ tsp	1½ tsp
Chopped candied peel	2 Tbs	2 Tbs
Chopped glacé cherries	2 Tbs	2 Tbs
Kirsch	2 Tbs	2 Tbs
Egg yolks	3	3
Gelatine, dissolved in 6 Tbs hot water	25g/1oz	1oz
Custard	250ml/8floz	1 cup
Double (heavy) cream, stiffly beaten	300ml/10floz	1¼ cups
Apricot jam	2 Tbs	2 Tbs

Preheat the oven to cool 150°C (Gas Mark 2, 300°F).

Put the rice, sugar, milk and vanilla in a well-greased baking dish and put the dish into the oven. Bake for 3 hours, or until the rice is cooked and all the liquid is absorbed.

Meanwhile, put the candied peel and glacé cherries in a bowl and pour over the kirsch. Set aside to marinate at room temperature.

Remove the dish from the oven and gradually beat in the egg yolks, then the gelatine. Set aside to cool for 15 minutes.

Beat in the fruit and kirsch mixture, then fold in the custard and cream.

Lightly coat the inside of a 1¼l/2 pint (1½ quart) mould with the jam. Pour the rice mixture into the mould, smoothing it down. Put into the refrigerator to chill for 2 hours, or until the rice has set.

CHARLOTTE AUX MARRONS
(Chestnut Mould)

The original charlotte was 'invented' by the great Carême, but since his original (charlotte russe), there have been many superlative variations on the theme—this one uses chestnuts, a flavouring very popular with the French.

	Metric/U.K.	U.S.
Milk	225ml/7floz	⅞ cup
Water	75ml/3floz	⅜ cup
Sponge finger biscuits (lady-fingers)	30	30
Sugar	75g/3oz	⅜ cup
Gelatine, dissolved in 4 Tbs hot water	15g/½oz	½oz
Canned unsweetened chestnut purée	165g/5½oz	5½oz
Orange-flavoured liqueur	2 Tbs	2 Tbs
Canned preserved chestnuts	125g/4oz	4oz
Double (heavy) cream	300ml/10floz	1¼ cups

Line the bottom of a 1¼l/2 pint (1½ quart) mould with a circle of greaseproof or waxed paper. Set aside.

Mix together 75ml/3floz (⅜ cup) each of the milk and water. One by one, dip the biscuits (cookies) into the mixture, coating them well, but being careful not to saturate them. Line the sides of the mould with the biscuits (cookies), reserving the extra to use later. Trim the biscuits (cookies) to fit the top of the mould. Set aside.

Dissolve the sugar in the remaining milk, stirring constantly until it has dissolved. Stir in the dissolved gelatine, then the chestnut purée and orange-flavoured liqueur. Remove the pan from the heat and transfer the mixture to a bowl. Chill in the refrigerator for 30 minutes, or until the mixture is beginning to set.

Sumptuous Charlotte aux Marrons—a superb combination of chestnut purée, cream and orange-flavoured liqueur, all moulded together.

The French make apple tart differently from everybody else, but the result is just as delicious, as this Tarte aux Pommes testifies.

Drain the preserved chestnuts, reserving the syrup. Chop coarsely and set aside. Beat the cream until it is thick but not stiff. Beat half the cream into the gelatine mixture, then fold in the remaining cream. Fold in the chopped chestnuts.

Spoon the mixture into the lined mould. Arrange the remaining biscuits (cookies) over the top, to cover the mould completely, and trim off any protruding parts.

Cover with greaseproof or waxed paper and chill in the refrigerator for at least 6 hours or overnight.

To serve, remove the paper and run a knife around the edge of the mould. Invert on to a serving dish, giving a sharp shake. The charlotte should slide out easily.

Pour over the reserved chestnut syrup and serve at once.

10 Servings

CREPES SUZETTE
(Crêpes Flambéed with Grand Marnier)

This is one of the most famous of all French desserts and its range of popularity is such that it can be found on the menu of the most elegant restaurants in the country—and yet it is also, traditionally, served from street stalls all over Paris. If you prefer, use all Grand Marnier rather than mixing it with brandy.

	Metric/U.K.	U.S.
Crêpe batter (sweet) (page 64)	150g/5oz	$\frac{5}{8}$ cup
Medium oranges	2	2
Sugar cubes	4	4
Castor (super fine) sugar	50g/2oz	$\frac{1}{4}$ cup
Unsalted butter, softened	175g/6oz	12 Tbs

	Metric/U.K.	U.S.
Fresh orange juice	75ml/3floz	$\frac{3}{8}$ cup
Grand Marnier	5 Tbs	5 Tbs
Brandy	3 Tbs	3 Tbs

Fry the crêpes according to the instructions in the basic recipe. Keep hot.

Rub each orange all over with the sugar cubes to extract the zest from the rind. Put the sugar into a bowl and crush with the back of a wooden spoon. Peel the oranges, discarding any pith. Chop the rind very finely and add to the sugar. Stir in half the castor (superfine) sugar and the softened butter. Cream the mixture until it is light and fluffy. Stir in the orange juice, then 3 tablespoons of the Grand Marnier and beat until the mixture is well blended and creamy.

Melt the orange butter in a frying-pan. Holding the outer edges of a crêpe with your fingertips, dip it into the butter mixture until it is well soaked. Carefully fold in half, then in quarters. Transfer to a warmed serving dish. Repeat until all the crêpes have been well coated. Sprinkle over the remaining sugar and pour over any remaining melted butter.

Warm the remaining Grand Marnier and brandy together until they are hot. Pour over the crêpes and ignite, shaking the dish gently and carefully. When the flames die away, serve at once.

4-6 Servings

MOUSSE AU CHOCOLAT
(Chocolate Mousse)

For the best results make this dessert the day before you wish to serve it and chill in the refrigerator. As a finishing touch, decorate with grated chocolate and/or whipped cream.

	Metric/U.K.	U.S.
Dark cooking (semi-sweet) chocolate, broken into small pieces	225g/8oz	8 squares
Strong black coffee	3 Tbs	3 Tbs
Unsalted butter, cut into small pieces	40g/1½oz	3 Tbs
Eggs, separated	4	4
Brandy	2 Tbs	2 Tbs

Combine the chocolate and coffee in a heat-proof bowl. Put the bowl over a saucepan half-filled with hot water and set the pan over moderately low heat. Cook the mixture, beating constantly with a wooden spoon, until the chocolate has melted and the mixture is smooth.

Beat in the butter, a few pieces at a time, and continue beating until it is thoroughly blended. Add the egg yolks and cook, beating constantly, for 5 minutes, or until the mixture has thickened and is smooth. Do not let the mixture come to the boil.

Remove the pan from the heat and the bowl from the pan. Stir in the brandy and set the mixture aside for 30 minutes to cool completely.

Meanwhile, beat the egg whites until they form stiff peaks. Quickly fold the egg whites into the chocolate mixture.

Spoon the mousse into individual serving glasses and chill for 4 hours, or overnight.

6 Servings

TARTE AUX POMMES
(Apple Flan)

	Metric/U.K.	U.S.
Shortcrust pastry dough	175g/6oz	6oz
Thick sweet apple purée	300ml/10floz	1¼ cups
Dessert apples, cored, peeled and thinly sliced	½kg/1lb	1lb
Grated rind and juice of ½ lemon		
Redcurrant or apple jelly	4 Tbs	4 Tbs
Brandy	2 Tbs	2 Tbs

Preheat the oven to fairly hot 200°C (Gas Mark 6, 400°F).

Roll out the pastry dough to about ½cm/¼in thick and use it to line a well-greased 23cm/9in flan tin. Put the flan tin on a baking sheet.

Spoon the apple purée over the bottom of the case to cover it completely, then arrange the apple slices on top, in concentric circles. Sprinkle over the lemon rind and juice.

Put the baking sheet into the oven and bake the flan for 40 to 45 minutes, or until the pastry and apples are cooked. Remove from the oven and set aside to cool.

Warm the jelly and brandy together until the jelly has dissolved. Brush the glaze gently over the apples and serve the flan warm or cold.

6 Servings

PROFITEROLES AUX GLACES
(Choux Puffs with Ice-Cream)

	Metric/U.K.	U.S.
PASTRY		
Water	300ml/10floz	1¼ cups
Butter, cut into small pieces	75g/3oz	6 Tbs
Salt	1 tsp	1 tsp
Pinch of grated nutmeg		
Flour	275g/10oz	2½ cups
Large eggs	5	5
Egg, beaten with ½ tsp water		
FILLING		
Vanilla ice-cream	450ml/15floz	2 cups
Dark cooking (semi-sweet) chocolate, melted	125g/4oz	4 squares

Bring the water to the boil in a large saucepan. Add the butter, salt and nutmeg and, when the butter has melted, remove from the heat and gradually beat in the flour. Continue beating until the dough comes away from the sides of the pan.

One by one, beat the eggs into the mixture, making sure each is absorbed before adding the next. When the eggs have been added, the mixture should be thick and glossy.

Preheat the oven to hot 220°C (Gas Mark 7, 425°F). Lightly grease two baking sheets.

Fill a forcing bag, fitted with a plain nozzle, with the pastry dough. Squeeze the dough on to the baking sheets in circular mounds (about 5cm/2in in diameter and 2½cm/1in in height). If you do not have a forcing bag, arrange the dough carefully into mounds on the sheets, using two spoons. The puffs will expand considerably in baking, so allow plenty of space between each one. Coat each puff with the beaten egg mixture and put the sheets into the oven. Bake for 10 minutes. Reduce the oven temperature to fairly hot 190°C (Gas Mark 5, 375°F) and bake the puffs for a further 25 to 30 minutes, or until they have doubled in size and are light brown in colour.

Remove from the oven and make a slit in the side of each puff to allow the steam to escape. Replace the puffs in the turned-off oven for 10 minutes, then transfer to a wire rack to cool to room temperature.

Cut the tops off the puffs and reserve. Fill the puffs with the ice-cream. Replace the tops and arrange the filled puffs on a serving dish.

One of the classic French pastries, with a luscious filling—Profiteroles, puffs of choux pastry baked, then filled with ice-cream and topped with chocolate sauce.

Pour over the melted chocolate and serve at once.

8 Large Puffs

MADELEINES
(Shell-Shaped Sponges)

The invention of the madeleine is generally attributed to one of the great early pastry cooks, Avice, who was in the service of Prince Talleyrand. It has remained a popular part of the French culinary experience ever since, and has even been immortalized in literature—it was the action of biting into a madeleine which caused the hero of Proust's Remembrances of Things Past to remember . . . To be traditionally correct, the cakes should be baked in special moulds; they will, however, taste just as nice if cooked in ordinary muffin tins, even if the shapes aren't strictly 'shell'!

	Metric/U.K.	U.S.
Butter, melted	125g/4oz plus 2 Tbs	8 Tbs plus 2 Tbs
Flour, sifted	125g/4oz plus 2 Tbs	1 cup plus 2 Tbs
Castor (superfine) sugar	125g/4oz	½ cup
Eggs	4	4
Vanilla essence (extract)	½ tsp	½ tsp

Preheat the oven to fairly hot 200°C (Gas Mark 6, 400°F). Lightly grease 36 madeleine moulds with the 2 tablespoons of butter. Sprinkle the moulds with the 2 tablespoons of flour, tipping and rotating to distribute it evenly, and knocking out any excess.

Beat the sugar, eggs and vanilla together until the mixture is very thick. Very gradually, fold in the remaining flour. Add the remaining butter until it is thoroughly mixed. Spoon the batter into the moulds until they are about three-quarters full. Put the moulds on a baking sheet and put the sheet into the oven. Bake for 7 to 10 minutes, or until a skewer inserted into the centres of the cakes comes out clean.

Remove from the oven and leave the cakes to cool in the moulds for 5 minutes before turning out on to a wire rack to cool completely. Serve cold.

36 Cakes